THE BRITISH ACADEMY

The Early Poetry of Israel in its Physical and Social Origins

By

George Adam Smith, D.D., LL.D., Litt.D.

Principal and Vice-Chancellor of the University of Aberdeen
Formerly Professor of Old Testament Language, Literature, and Theology, United Free Church College, Glasgow

The Schweich Lectures

1910

WIPF & STOCK · Eugene, Oregon

Wipf and Stock Publishers
199 W 8th Ave, Suite 3
Eugene, OR 97401

The Early Poetry of Israel in its Physical and Social Origins
The Schweich Lectures 1910
By Smith, George Adam
ISBN 13: 978-1-60608-243-0
Publication date 11/21/2008
Previously published by Oxford University Press, 1912

TO

L. S.

CONTENTS

PREFACE

THESE three Lectures with their Introduction were delivered in London before the British Academy towards the close of 1910, but till this summer I have been unable to prepare them for the press. In the Introduction I recount the materials available for the illustration of the subject; but it was not possible to cover the whole range of these within three hours. I have, therefore, much to add to what was actually spoken. Some of the discussion of technical questions in Lecture I required expansion; and I desired to give in Lecture III as full a translation as was possible of all the poetical passages relevant to the subject.

Where it is necessary to quote the original I have done so, for the sake of those who are ignorant of Hebrew, in the letters of our own alphabet. The details of this transliteration are given on page 1 and at the top of page 4; I may say here that in the transliteration of single words in Lecture III and its notes, I have not thought it necessary always to mark the softer forms of the letters *b*, *g*, *d*, *k*, *p*, and *t*. The name of the God of Israel is given as Yahweh, except in the translation of Deborah's song, where, as in our English version, it appears as The LORD.

What is said on pages 84, 85 as to the translation of the Song of Deborah, and the division of it into lines, and its rhythms, is applicable to all the translations offered in these Lectures.

In connection with the discussion of rhythms and parallelism in Lecture I, the reader should consult Professor G. B. Gray's paragraphs (44–57) on 'The Poetical Forms of the Prophetic Literature' in his 'Commentary on the Book of Isaiah, i–xxxix', in the *International Critical Commentary*, 1912. The volume by Professor Gordon, of Montreal, on *The Poets of the Old Testament* (1912), has reached me only this month, and I regret that I have not been able to make use of the valuable materials for translation which it contains.

I reserve the right to use the contents of these Lectures in a larger work on Hebrew poetry which I hope some day to publish.

GEORGE ADAM SMITH.

The University of Aberdeen.
October 1912.

INTRODUCTION

It requires but a slight acquaintance with the criticism of the Old Testament to appreciate the difficulty of stating the limits of our subject—'The Early Poetry of Israel'. We cannot be sure that all passages which are poetical in form as well as in spirit have as yet been detached from their environment of prose in the earlier literature of Israel; and again, the age of many of the poems or poetical fragments, which we may confidently distinguish as such, is still more uncertain.

For the purpose of the following Lectures I propose to use all pieces which are generally and reasonably—though not always conclusively—assigned to the centuries before the eighth century B.C.: the age of the first prophets whose writings have come down to us, and probably the age of the bulk of those earliest documents of the Hexateuch, the so-called Jahwist and Elohist, in which most of the pieces have been preserved. That will include all the fragments of verse, mostly on genealogies and the characters and relations of tribes, which are found in the Book of Genesis, along with the fuller 'Blessing of Jacob' in chapter xlix and its counterpart (with differences) in Deuteronomy xxxiii; in Exodus xv, the Song of Miriam, and at least the opening of the Song of Moses, and xvii. 16, the War with Amalek; in Numbers the fragments found in chapters x. 35 36, xii. 6–8, xxi. 14^b 15, 17^b 18, 27–30[1]; and in chapters xxiii, xxiv the longer and shorter oracles of Balaam, the former of which I judge not later than David's time; in Joshua, the address to the Sun and Moon, x. 12 f.; in Judges, the Song of Deborah, ch. v, the Parable of the Trees, ch. ix, and the riddles and verses in the story of Samson, ch. xiv–xvi; in 1 Samuel the oracles in xv. 22 23 and 33, the repeated acclamation of David, xviii. 7, xxi. 12, xxix. 5, and the 'mashal' in xxiv. 14[2]; in 2 Samuel the elegies ascribed to David, i. 17 ff., iii. 33 f.[3]; and in 1 Kings, viii. 12 f. (after the Septuagint) and xii. 16. Some of these are cited by the prose documents, which have preserved them, as taken from two or three early collections of songs: 'The Book of the Upright

[1] The fragments in Lev. x. 3 and Num. vi. 24–26 have come down to us in the Priestly Document of later date. Their date is unknown. [2] English, verse 13.

[3] The dates of xxii (= Ps. xviii) and xxiii. 1–7 are more doubtful.

or Valiant' (?),[1] 'The Book of the Wars of Yahweh',[2] and 'The Book of the Song *or* Songs'.[3] The presence of other poems in the earlier Books may be due to the same collections.

With all these pieces, most of which are embodied in works not later than the eighth century, we might take a number of popular songs and proverbs quoted by the prophets, which, though we cannot tell their date, are as primitive in character as the undoubtedly earlier poems.

But I shall also use from poems which are obviously later than the eighth century, like 'The Song of Moses' in Deuteronomy xxxii, such portions as reflect the desert circumstance of Israel's younger days and the social changes which the nation underwent on their settlement to agriculture. And, of course, I shall not hesitate to draw comparisons and illustrations, especially of the subject of the first lecture, from the rest of Hebrew literature.

It is hard for us who speak English to regard the poetry of the Hebrews with a single eye. It lies before us in a double perspective.

In one aspect it is the nearest poetry of all, the first which we learned; through the open windows of which we had our earliest visions of time, of space, of eternity, and of God. Its rhythms haunt our noblest prose; its lyrics are our most virile and enduring hymns.

But in another perspective, which has only recently been cleared for us, Hebrew poetry lies very far away: the product of an alien race and of a stage of culture distant from our own. The poetries, hitherto studied by the large majority of my hearers, lie within the Aryan race, practically within Europe. They are from civilisations out of which our own has grown; and in languages which have almost exactly our alphabet, and some of which we call classic because the canons of their literature rule the logic and the rhetoric of our own. In particular, most of these Aryan languages hold in common the words Poet and Poetry: by which they understand the twin faculties of Imagination that 'bodies forth the forms of things unknown', and of verbal construction and melody in the presentation of these forms. But the subject of our present Lectures leads us among another race, not only with a somewhat different alphabet, which implies a somewhat different voice and ear than ours; nor only without some combinations of sound which we count the more musical;

[1] Sepher hay-Yashar, Joshua x. 13, 2 Sam. i. 18.

[2] Sepher Milḥᵃmōth Yahweh, Num. xxi. 14.

[3] Sepher hash-Shīr, 1 Kings viii. 53, LXX; perhaps a corruption of the above S. hay-Yashar.

but with the imagination and the constructive ability, which for us give the Poet his name, less developed, less sustained. Indeed, we leave the name itself behind us. Those who among the Hebrews correspond to the Aryan poets call themselves singers, minstrels, shepherds of words, comparers, bewailers, and the like—anything but makers. The verbs which describe their functions express not the power of creation but the capacity for impression: not the art of building or of ornament so much as the process of outpouring and the spirit of urgency. The singers rose from and were inspired by less coherent forms of life than our own, and this social looseness, along with their people's ignorance of architecture and other constructive arts, has had its effect on their poetry.

These things will be explained and illustrated in the course of the Lectures. In the first I propose to deal with the Language, Structure and Rhythms of the Poetry.

THE EARLY POETRY OF ISRAEL IN ITS PHYSICAL AND SOCIAL ORIGINS

LECTURE I

LANGUAGE, STRUCTURE AND RHYTHMS

1. Language.

In appreciating the Hebrew language as a vehicle for poetry, we must first reckon with the fact, already mentioned, that its alphabet is somewhat different from our own. The differences consist (1) in the use of consonants, and of varieties of consonants, strange to our ears and difficult to our organs of speech; along with the prevalence of several consonants, especially gutturals, which we count among the less musical; (2) in the absence of some combinations of consonants, which to us are melodious and dear; and (3) in the peculiar relation to the consonants of the vowels, which are not integral to the root as in Aryan languages, which were not marked in the earlier script, and the tradition of which was therefore far less certain than that of our own.

Of our gutturals Hebrew had all except the composite *kw* or *qu*, the velar or shrouded guttural, and *x*, a composite guttural and sibilant. But in addition to ours the alphabet contains the light breathing, *'Aleph* ('), inaudible at the beginning of a word, and sensible in the middle only when it breaks between two vowels; *'Ayin* ('), formed by a curious and difficult check on the breath at the bottom of the windpipe, with probably (as in Arabic but under the same sign) a variation approaching the *gr* of some Frenchmen; *Qoph* or the deeper *k* (*ḳ*); at least two and possibly three degrees of the letter *h*.

As in other Semitic languages so in Hebrew the gutturals prevail to an extent which is as harsh to our ear as the lavish sibilants of English to an Italian. Here are three instances taken at random, lines of ordinary words into which there has been no intentional intrusion of gutturals. The vowels printed above the line are very fugitive sounds. Final *h* is not sounded except when it has a point beneath it, and *h* after *b*, *g*, *d*, *k*, *p*, and *t* simply indicates the softer forms of these letters. In Hebrew the accent is nearly always on the last syllable.

Gen. xxvii. 27, 29, from Isaac's Blessing of Jacob—

R^{e}'eh re^{a}ḥ b^{e}nī
K^{e}re^{a}ḥ sadheh male'
'Ashĕr ber^{a}khọ̄ Yahweh
H^{e}weh gh^{e}bhīr l^{e}'ăḥĕkha
'Or^{a}rĕkha 'arūr um^{e}bhar^{a}khĕkha barukh.

Gen. xlix. 8, from Jacob's Blessing of Judah—

Y^{e}hūdhah ’ăttah yōdhūkha ’aḥĕkha
Yadh^{e}kha b^{e}ʻórĕph ’oy^{e}bhĕkha
Yishtaḥ^{a}wū l^{e}kha b^{e}nē ’abhīkha.

Deut. xxxiii. 26, from the Song of Moses—

’Ēn k^{e}’el Y^{e}shŭrūn
Rōkhebh shamáïm b^{e}ʻĕzrékha
Ubh^{e}gha’^{a}wathō sh^{e}ḥaḳīm
M^{e}ʻonah ’^{e}lohē ḳédhem
Umittáḥăth z^{e}roʻōth ʻōlam.

Or the contrast may be put in this way. In the English couplet from the Song of Debōrah—

Was shield seen or lance
In the forty thousands of Israel?—

no gutturals occur and six sibilants (besides *th*); but the Hebrew has only one sibilant and three gutturals besides five alephs—

Maghēn ’im-yera’ĕh w^{e}rómaḥ
B^{e}’arbaʻīm ’élĕph b^{e}yisra’el.

Again, a triplet from the same song in English—

Riding roan asses,
Sitting on rugs (?),
Walking the highways—sing them!—

has six sibilants and three gutturals; while the Hebrew—

Rōkh^{e}bhē ’^{a}thonoth ṣ^{e}ḥorōth
Yosh^{e}bhē ʻal-middīn
W^{e}hol^{e}khē ʻal-dérĕkh sīḥūm—

has eight gutturals besides one aleph, and only three pure sibilants besides *th* twice.[1]

These are ordinary lines, but when as in some passages of the prophets the speaker gives himself up to denounce or to imprecate, his lines are packed with words still more full of gutturals. In Hebrew, *to call with the throat*[2] is to speak with vehemence. The dry climate and large leisure of the East bestow on the lower chords of the voice a greater depth and suppleness; and Orientals have elaborated their throat-letters to a number unmarked in any Western alphabet.

How delicately the Hebrews distinguished their many gutturals may be seen not only from the variety of these, but from the way in

[1] It must be remembered, however, that in their use of assonance Hebrew poets made sometimes a lavish use of sibilants. See the Song of Lamech, and the citation from Isaiah below, p. 7.

[2] קרא בגרון.

which in inflection and declension the standard vowels are modified by neighbouring gutturals. There is, too, an extraordinary beauty in the mingling of the softer gutturals with the liquids, by which Hebrew poets have produced some of the gentlest measures heard in any literature. As in Ps. xxiii. 1, 2—

Yahwéh my Shepherd, I lack not,
By waters of rest He doth lead me.

Yahweh Roʿī lo-ʾĕḥsar
ʿAl-mē m^{e}nūḥōth y^{e}naḥ^{a}lenī.

Or in Ps. xliii. 3, 5—

Send out Thy light and Thy troth,
  They be that lead me!
Why dost thou give in, O my soul,
  And be moaning upon me?
Hold thou to God, for yet shall I praise Him,
  My Courage, my God!

Sh^{e}lăḥ ʾōr^{e}kha wăʾ^{a}mitt^{e}kha
  Hemmah yan^{e}ḥūnī
Mah tishtoḥ^{a}ḥī naphshī
  Ūmah tĕh^{e}mī ʿalai
Hōḥīlī le'lohīm kī-ʿōdh ʾōdhĕnnū
  Y^{e}shuʿath-panaī we'lohaī.

Or the incomparable melody which breaks upon exiled Israel, Isa. xl. 1—

Comfort ye, comfort my people,
  Sayeth your God.

Naḥ^{a}mū n'aḥ^{a}mū ʿammī
  Yōmar ʾ^{e}lohēkhem.

It would be hard to find in any language lips that more gently woo the broken heart. I do not know whether Handel had heard the original, but he has caught the very music in the bars with which his *Messiah* opens.

Hebrew has been deemed deficient in liquids, and indeed is without the musical *ng*. But *l* and *n* (and *r*) are as frequent as with ourselves. It is of great advantage to the music to have duals and plurals in *im* (where we, alas! have almost only *s*), some verbal forms in *un*, and, for the frequent preposition *to*, the letter *l* as a prefix.

Of our dentals and sibilants Hebrew has all except *j* or soft *g*, the want of which is hardly a disadvantage. Besides *sh* and a sharper form of *s* it adds the palatal *ṣ* and *ṭ*. Like the deeper *ḳ* these are real additions to its musical resources.

Of the explosives *b* and *p* much use was made by the poets. After vowels, *b*, *g*, *d*, *k*, *p* and *t* are all soft—*bh*, *gh*, *dh*, *kh*, *ph* or *f*, and *th*—except when they are doubled, in which case they remain hard. *v* was probably soft like *w*, as in modern Arabic; and there was also the weak consonant, which we signify by *y* and the Germans by *j*.

I take next the combination of consonants.

Like most Orientals the Hebrews avoided pronouncing two consonants together at the beginning of a syllable. A native of the Nearer East can hardly open a syllable with a couple of consonants. Either he slips a furtive vowel between the two, which in Hebrew, however, *does not count as a syllable*; or he prefixes a full vowel with the so-called 'prosthetic 'Aleph' and creates another syllable. Thus he pronounces Protestant B^{e}rootestantī, and Scotland 'Iskotalandī. Similarly the Jew of the time of Augustus or of Hadrian transferred to his own language the Greek *προσθήκη* as pardasḳ^{e}ya; *πρεσβυτής* as p^{e}ruzbuṭī; and *praepositus* as p^{e}ruphsīṭos; but *στολή* as 'isṭ^{e}la and *στρατηγός* as 'isṭarṭigh, with the 'prosthetic 'Aleph'. He also separated the frequent *x* of Greek, as in 'aghistaryon for *ἐξιτήριον*, or when it was initial he compassed it by a 'prosthetic 'Aleph', as in 'akhs^{e}na for *ξένος*.[1]

Perhaps to the same inability is due the absence of *-ng*, and of the velar guttural *qu* which is the charm of some of our most musical words: queen, quest, quiet, and requiem. A Hebrew could have uttered the last by dividing the syllables between the *q* and the *w*. But it is not probable that at the beginning of a syllable he ever took the guttural and the *w* together; for either the *w* would become a vowel, or he would slip a furtive vowel in before it. Instead of queen, quiet, quire, and quest, imagine k^{e}ween, k^{e}wiet, k^{e}wire, k^{e}west, and you can reckon the music lost to his language, and lost, it would seem, by so little. This characteristic insertion of the light, quick 'sheva', 'the volatilised vowel,' as it has been called, suffices to break that grip of consonant by consonant which is the strength of some of our finest words—brow, brother, breast, grand, crash, prince, stream, strain. For as no vowels can do, such bracing of consonants gives the full phonetic value of strength, of pressure, of construction; or when followed by a long vowel, renders the effect of obtrusion or explosion; or with the softer consonants sends speech forth like the flowing of a stream, or like a flag flung on the breeze. The Hebrew could *close* a syllable on two strong consonants, yet even here he was given to slipping a short vowel between them.[2] But

Other instances are p^{e}rōzdōr for *πρόσοδος*, p^{e}rōḳhōphī for *προκοπή*; '^{a}garma for *γραμμάριον*, and 'ist^{e}lī for *στήλη*. There are scores of others.

[2] As in the segholates of the 2nd decl. Cf. Dalman, *Paläst. Diwan*, xxxiv.

it cannot be too often repeated that the furtive vowel does not make a syllable, and we shall find that in verse it often disappears.

On the other hand the Hebrew made a strenuous use of the doubled consonant, which, though it survives in our script, we have almost wholly lost in speech. The Hebrew could not lose it, for the duplication of a radical consonant was a cardinal factor in his grammar: rendering to his verbs, for example, an intensive or a factitive force. Thus shabhar with the single soft *b* is *break*, but shibbēr *break in pieces, shatter*; gadhal is *grow great*, but giddēl *make great, exalt*; lamadh *learn*, but limmēdh *teach*. Sometimes this form with the doubled letter is used wholly instead of, or partly in preference to, the simple form, without any purpose of intensifying the meaning or giving it a factitive turn, but only in order to bring out and enforce the music of the word and of the action it describes: as in the two verbs for *sing*, hallēl and rinnēn. By this duplication of his liquids the Hebrew atoned somewhat for his want of our ringing *-ng*.

The assimilation of a neighbouring liquid is another cause of the doubled consonant; as, for example, Yitten for yinten, and the absorption by the initial consonants in nouns of the final *l* of the preceding definite article.[1] Still another cause was the licence of the poets, who not infrequently doubled a consonant where in prose it is not doubled. Obviously this was done for musical reasons, in order to increase the stresses on a line or to shift them or otherwise to alter the time or measure.[2]

But whatever may have been the causes of the doubled consonant, the Hebrew poet availed himself of it as the Greek did, yet more lavishly, for emphasis and urgency, for the impression of weight and mass, or for lingering melody. Let me give some examples, which both illustrate the musical value of the doubled letter in Hebrew, and by their translations expose the difficulty of echoing that music in our own language with its far less frequent use of the device. At the same time even English has some possibilities left in this direction,[3] and I have chosen for the translations as many words with doubled consonants as I could find for a fair reproduction of the meaning. Where these have failed me I have sought equivalents for the Hebrew doubled letter in English words that have braced consonants.

[1] Here again we see how the Hebrew avoided as far as possible the pronunciation of two different consonants together.

[2] See below, p. 19.

[3] e.g. glad and gladden.

The first illustration is from the Song of Deborah.[1]

’Az hull^{e}mu[2] ‘ikk^{e}bhē susīm
Dah^{a}rōth dah^{a}rōth ’abbīrau.

Then thudded the hoofs of the horses,
Plunge upon plunge of his stallions.

The next[3] tells how a great crowd was drawn into the order and melody of a solemn march, its praise billowing up to the Temple. An exile, torn from his country, remembers—

How I passed through the throng, headed them,
  On to God’s-house,
To the call of song and of praise,
  Surges of worship!

Kī’ e‘^{e}bhor bassakh ’ĕddaddem
  ‘Adh bēth-’^{e}lohīm
B^{e}ḳōl-rinnah w^{e}thodhah
  Hamōn ḥōghegh.

Or take the solemn prayer[4]—

Suffice us betimes with Thy mercy,
That we sing and be glad all our days.
Gladden, for days Thou hast stunned, us.

Sabb^{e}‘ēnū babbōḳĕr ḥasd^{e}kha
Ūn^{e}rann^{e}nah ūnism^{e}ḥah b^{e}khŏl-yomēnū
Samm^{e}ḥenū kīmōth ‘innīthanū.

It is, however, for the crashing and reverberation of the sea, or of the peoples in tumult, that the doubled consonant, now an explosive or sibilant, is used to its finest effects. The English plurals *many waters* and *many peoples* are weak in sound; they trickle rather than surge. But for the first Hebrew has maīm rabbīm, and for the second ‘ammīm rabbīm and l^{e}’ummīm rabbīm.

Take Ps. xciii. 4—

Than voices of waters immense,
More majestic than breakers of ocean,
Majestic on high Yahwéh.

Mikḳōlōth maīm rabbīm
’Addīr mimmishb^{e}rē-yam
’Addīr bammarōm Yahweh.

Or the passage in which Isaiah has by long vowels rendered the slow lift and roll of the billows, but by doubled consonants their

[1] Judges v. 22.

[2] So probably we should read (after LXX, Theod., and Vulgate) instead of halemu.

[3] Ps. xlii. 5.

[4] Ps. xc. 15.

distant booming; and then, as they are checked, their crash and hissing sweep along the Syrian coast (Isa. xvii. 12, 13). He is using this as a figure of the vain tumult of the peoples against the God of Israel—

Hōi h^{a}mōn ʿammīm rabbīm
Kah^{a}mōth yammīm yeh^{e}māyūn
Ush^{e}’ọ̄n l^{e}’ummīm kabbīrīm
Kish^{e}ʿōn maīm yishsha’ūn
L^{e}’ummim kish^{e}’ōn maīm rabbīm yishsha’ūn
W^{e}ghaʿar bō w^{e}nas mimmerḥaḳ
W^{e}ruddaph k^{e}moṣ-harīm liphne-ru^{a}ḥ
Ukh^{e}ghalgal liphne-suphah.

Woe, the booming of peoples multitudinous!
As the booming of seas are they booming;
And the crash of nations immense,[1]
As the crash of waters are crashing;
[Nations—as the crash of great waters are crashing,]
But he chides it, it fleeth afar,
Chased as chaff of the hills by the wind,
As dust-rings[2] in front of the storm.

I am aware that even so grand a reflection of the surge and tumult of the sea fails in the rhythm and flexibility with which more than one Aryan language has echoed it all.

Some ears may feel, too, that in all these poems the doubled letter tends to increase the staccato effect of which I have spoken. But on the other hand it gives the voice something to grip and roll upon: for grief and scorn, or the emphasis of hate; for solemn prayer and struggling hope; or for the ringing forth of joy and triumph.

2. Structure.

Passing from the alphabet, I have time only to note those features of the Hebrew Vocabulary and of the Syntax which bear upon style and rhythm.

The Vocabulary has two wants: the want, especially in the earlier stages of the language, of abstract terms, and the want throughout of compound words; neither of which, be it remarked in passing, is a disadvantage to the kinds of poetry most prevalent in Hebrew. Hebrew words express things or actions rather than ideas. Even the adjectives are not abstractions of qualities or colours, but are derived from the names of concrete objects which possess or produce these. The

[1] Kabbirim, *mighty* or *immense*, stands in the text in the fourth line with *waters* but obviously belongs to *nations* in the third line: cf. the Greek. The fifth line is elided by many as due to dittography. But see on the swell-verse, p. 20.

[2] Or rolling thistles.

art of compounding words, so natural to the Greeks and other Aryans, was almost unknown to the Hebrew. It has been calculated that while Greek has 100,000 words but only 1,800 roots, Hebrew has actually 2,000 roots, or 200 more than Greek, yet only 10,000 words, or one-tenth of the Greek. If this be correct, Greek has 50 times, but Hebrew only 5 times, as many words as it has roots. Hebrew words are still sonorous with the sound or vibrant with the feeling that instinctively called them forth. They are little advanced beyond the root stage. In comparison with Greek or Latin words they look both undeveloped and undressed, with a sameness in spite of all their rugged differences, like the sameness of stones in a brook. And this impression of simplicity is strengthened by the disappearance of the ancient case-endings of the nouns.

Further, as Emanuel Deutsch pointed out,[1] 'the Semitic idiom is bereft of that infinite variety of little words, particles, conjunctions, auxiliary verbs, &c., which, ready for any emergency, like so many living links imperceptibly bind word to word, phrase to phrase, and period to period, which indeed are the very life and soul of what is called Construction.'

The Syntax, too, is simple; the sentence is a straightforward statement. Co-ordination of sentences is the prevailing rule, and there are comparatively few forms of the subordinate clause. 'Compare with this', as Deutsch again well says, 'the suppleness of the Aryan languages and that boundless supply of aids that enable them to produce the most telling combinations on the spur of the moment, their exquisitely consummate and refined syntactical development that can change, shift, and alter the position of word and phrase and sentence and period to almost any place so as to give force to any part of their speech.'[2]

Consider these features and you will appreciate the type of architecture essential to the Hebrew language. Contrasted with that of the Greek, it is like building with the stones of the field to building with dressed and ornamented ashlar from the quarry. In reading a Hebrew poem I am often reminded of the Law: *If thou wilt make Me an altar of stones, thou shalt not build it of dressed stones.*[3] The metaphor is hardly sufficient. For as you read Hebrew poems you feel that the words in their rough shapes and loose connections are not at all building-material; but are rather missiles like the pebbles from the brook with which David filled his wallet when he went out against the giant. It is their separate weight and speed, their hissing

[1] *Literary Remains*, p. 301. [2] loc. cit. [3] Exod. xx. 22.

through the air, their impingement and penetration, which strike the ear.

But out of this springs a consequence important to ourselves who speak the English language. From what I have been saying it is obvious that to translate Hebrew into Greek or Latin is to run its music into moulds less fitted for them than the Anglo-Saxon used by Cædmon for his paraphrases, or the English of the authors of our 'authorized' and earlier versions. In Cædmon's poems on the Old Testament we find a dialect less constructive, melodious and august than Latin or Greek, which nevertheless by these very defects is more sympathetic to the original than they can be. Nor does the later English lose this advantage, but rather adds to it. For, as Dr. Johnson remarks, the change from Anglo-Saxon to English was effected less by the introduction of new words than by the simplification of old ones. Syllables were cut off, terminations were softened, and, as in Hebrew, case-endings disappeared. Therefore we may dare to say that readers of the English Old Testament get nearer to the temper of the music, nearer to the exact rhythm of Hebrew poetry than did the Hellenistic Jews of Alexandria with the Septuagint, or the mediaeval Latins through the Vulgate.

A confirmation of these remarks on the temper and structure of the Hebrew language is found in the terms by which it describes speech, poetry and song. Almost none of these betray an instinct for order or construction.

The Hebrews had the idea, common to all languages, of speech as a *counting* or *telling*:

Hash-shamaim m^{e}sapp^{e}rim k^{e}bhodh-'El
The heavens are telling the glory of God.[1]

Of the two commonest words for *speak* 'Amar has the radical sense of making prominent or salient: indicate, elicit, make a thing speak for itself; while Dibber, if we may judge from the use of the root in Hebrew and other Semitic languages to express leading or driving,[2] appears to describe speech as the shepherding of words. The metaphor is natural to a race of nomadic shepherds, and appropriately renders the loose arrangement of their style. Nabha', to bubble or gurgle out (probably also nabha'), and sī^{a}ḥ (originally to be

[1] Ps. xix. 2 (A.V. 1).

[2] Arab. dabara, *to come behind* (cf. Heb. d^{e}bhīr, *back*); Syr. debir, to guide cattle or sheep, Heb. midhbar, the ground over which they are driven, pastoral (as distinct from arable) land; Ạram. dabara, guidance. In Arab. dabbara is to relate, and in Phoen., as in Heb., dabar is to speak. Compare Arabic sâk, to drive, cause to go, and then ask; sīyāk, intercessor; and fī sīāk el-kalam, in the course of the conversation. See, however, below p. 82 *n.* 2.

zealous [1]), haghah and zamam to croon, read, recite, n^{e}'um the prophetic oracle, millel to speak, hillel and rinnen to sing, are all immediate imitations of various sounds of the voice. Further, haghah and zamam illustrate the Oriental's difficulty to think except aloud. Massa', utterance or oracle, literally what rises or is uplifted, is derived either from the raising of the voice or from the sense of a burden and of responsibility in the message it carries. The etymology of shīr, song, is doubtful.[2] Of mashal and ʿanah I shall speak later.

The two verbs for sight, ḥazah, archaic and poetic, and ra'ah, the ordinary term, are both with their derivatives used of mental vision, as well as of the experiences of the ecstatic seer. In Hebrew there are even fair equivalents for *imagination*, which are so translated in our Versions: Yeṣer, literally *moulding*, then *purpose, imagination* (but also of images); and ḥashabh, to *think*, or account, with maḥ^{a}shabhah, applied both to the thoughts of God and to the devices or intentions of man. Kautzsch renders the combination of the two by 'Dichten und Trachten'. But the fact that these terms, when used of man, are throughout the Old Testament applied only to evil imaginations and thoughts in rebellion against God, except in two very late passages where they are used indifferently,[3] is a striking illustration of the great difference between the Hebrew idea of the Imagination and our own.

All these facts of the language and syntax warn us not to expect in Hebrew poetry the regular, intricate and delicate metres of the Aryan styles. We are dealing with a people originally nomadic and to the end unskilled in architecture or any elaborate art. The essential looseness of their life, visible in their language, was bound to affect the highest achievements of their literature. When they did concentrate their minds on utterance, their earnestness would appear less in a passion for beauty than in a sense of urgency and responsibility. Israel was a people of prophets rather than of poets.

[1] Nöldeke, *Z. D. M. G.* xxxvii. 537.

[2] Unless we seek the original meaning in the direction indicated by Shurah, a row or rank, especially of vines. Compare the Arabic sūr, a wall, and surah, in the plural, a line or stratum in a wall, but in the singular, a section or chapter in the Ḳoran. The Hebrew *sh-* corresponds regularly to the Arabic *s-*. Others relate the Hebrew shīr to the Arabic shiʿr.

[3] These two are 1 Chron. xxviii. 9, xxix. 18. As examples of the rest, where the words are used in an evil sense, take Gen. vi. 5, viii. 21; Deut. xxxi. 21; Ps. x. 2, cxl. 2; Prov. vi. 18; Lam. iii. 60, 61. Prov. vi. 18, xii. 20, &c., use ḥarash; Ps. ii. 1 ḥaghah, and Gen. xi. 6 zamam, in the sense of imagining.

3. Rhythms.

The earlier poetry of Israel has reached us embedded in prose and written as prose—that is, continuously and not in lines or stichoi. Some longer pieces have titles to indicate that they are songs; but many fragments are without this signal. How do we mark them as poetry? How do we divide them into lines of verse?

In the first place, of course, by the obvious signs by which in all literatures the form of poetry is distinguished from that of prose: to wit, an order of the words of a sentence different from the order normal in prose; numerous ellipses and compressions, and a preference for archaic words or forms of words, especially when these are more sonorous. In Hebrew poetry the verb does not always stand at the head of the clause, as is the rule in prose. The definite article, the relative, and some particles are often omitted. The suffixes to verbs and nouns, which are equivalent to our personal and possessive pronouns, as well as the terminations of some parts of the verb, appear in elongated and more musical forms. Proper names of high musical quality are placed in irregular but prominent positions. Rhyme, too, appears, though infrequently. These are the usual signs that a writing is not prose:[1] that the writer is aiming at poetical measure and music; that he is dividing his discourse into lines of verse.

And in fact, while the modifications of the forms of the words produce a melody greater than that of prose, the ellipses and compressions and the changed order of the words result in a distribution of the accents or stresses,[2] which proves the metrical character of the discourse and enables us to mark it off into more or less regular lines. Like the lines of all poetries in their earlier stages, each of these measures of Old Testament verse is a 'stop-line', a clause or sentence complete in itself. To this rule I have observed almost no exception in the poetry of our period. I need not give examples here. I have already given some, and will give many more.

The number of accents to the line varies. Some poems, or parts of poems, fall into a series of lines with only two stresses each;[3]

[1] Yet some of the prose writers in the Old Testament adopt for the sake of sonorousness one or other of these devices, but never rhyme.

[2] A century of research and debate has resulted in a pretty general agreement among scholars that it is accent or stress, and not the quantity of the syllables, which is the main factor in Hebrew metre. The student will find a full and clear history of the subject in Mr. W. H. Cobb's *A Criticism of Systems of Hebrew Metre* (Oxford, 1905).

[3] See parts of the Song of Deborah in Lecture III.

others into lines with three, others into lines with four. In all these the number of unaccented syllables varies, within limits of course, just as in those poetries of Europe of which the metre also depends on the proportion of the accents. In Hebrew words (so far as we know) the accent was almost invariably on the last syllable; occasionally it fell on the penultimate, but never before this. Yet in longer words with suffixes attached to them a minor or secondary emphasis was inevitable. As in modern European verse, contiguous monosyllables might each have an accent. But, as I shall have to emphasize later, we are still far from fully understanding the rules of Hebrew accentuation. All we can say is, that with regard to monosyllabic particles and some nominal constructions the practice appears to have varied, even within the same poem.

A signal advance in our knowledge of Hebrew rhythms was the discrimination [1] of the Ḳinah, or elegiac, measure, as it is called from its prevalence in the Book of Lamentations. This measure runs in alternately longer and shorter lines divided by a stop, the first with a rising, and the second with a falling cadence. The stresses are usually in the proportion of three to two.

But in every one of these measures, while the majority of lines have the normal proportion of stresses, there are frequent irregularities. A poem, the most of whose lines have three accents each, will be broken by several of two or four each; while sometimes a series perfectly regular in the proportion of their accents will be closed by a single longer line with an accent more than its predecessors.[2] In the Ḳinah rhythm the normal proportion of three to two is not always observed: we find couplets of four to three and four to two.

Such irregularities in the received text of the poems are regarded by a number of modern scholars as mere errors of the text, due to its imperfect tradition; and these scholars have proposed textual emendations with the view of reducing the poems to a perfect regularity of metre. It is true that many of the emendations are confirmed by the ancient versions of the Old Testament, and that they enhance either the sense, or the pith, or the music of the poetry. But for the vast majority of the proposed readings there is no external evidence; and a large proportion of them sadly flatten the ring or the swell of the verses.

I venture to think that such irregularities are capable of other explanations, and their first and principal cause appears to me to lie

[1] By Professor Budde: *Z. A. T. W.* 1882. [2] See below, p. 20.

in the dominant characteristic of Hebrew poetry—the Parallelism of its lines.[1]

In Hebrew poetry the clauses or sentences, which (as has been remarked) are universally, or almost universally, coincident with the rhythmic lines, stand in couplets, or less frequently in triplets, parallel in meaning to each other. In other words, the balance of music in the lines is wedded to—I think that it is controlled and modified by—a balance of thought and meaning. This parallelism is sometimes exact; the second line of the couplet, whether with or without verbal variations, does not carry the meaning further than the first has done. Sometimes it is progressive; the second line adds details to the idea of the first, or enforces it from another point of view, or carries it on to a fresh application. Sometimes the progress rises through three, or even four or five lines to a climax. Sometimes the parallelism is antithetic. And there is also a variety of the device, characteristic of the Psalms of Degrees, which merits the name rather of Spiralism than Parallelism, for by it the expression or development of the theme turns upon itself, and picks up and repeats some point or sound on which it has already dwelt. Before I continue the argument into which I have introduced Parallelism, it is needful to say something about the origins of this feature of many poetries.

Parallelism used to be regarded as the peculiar distinction of Hebrew poetry. But since the discovery of its prevalence in Babylonian, and in some forms of Egyptian, poetry, attempts have been made to derive it from one or other of those two civilisations, by which the literature and art of Israel were so profoundly affected in other directions. Parallelism, however, is not uncommon in the dialects of Semitic peoples more nearly akin to the Hebrews than even the Babylonians. So far as I know, there is not very much of it in the classical poetry of the nomad Arabs; nevertheless, among the virtues of style which Tha'alibi attributed to the Arab poet, Mutanabbi (915–65), is the fact that he divided his poetry into parallel sentences.[2] In the Palestine folk-songs of to-day Parallelism is frequent. I take the following instances translated from Professor Dalman's valuable collection[3]:—

Go now, my brother, and go,
  Go to the region of Ḥaleb.
Thou, the tattooed on the arms,
  Who forgest the necklace of gold!

[1] See Praelectio XIX of Bishop Lowth's *De Sacra Poesi Hebraeorum*, the classic passage on the subject, Eng. Translation by Gregory, London, 1847.

[2] See Nicholson, *A Literary History of the Arabs*, p. 311.

[3] *Palästinischer Diwan*, pp. 6, 7, 22.

Go now, my brother, and go,
  Go to the region of Muṣr,
Thou, the tattooed on the arms,
  Who forgest the necklace of coins.

Thou, that sleepest the sleep of the lamb,
  And the line on thy lips is sweet;
Were I not shy of my parents' face,
  I would run and would kiss thee asleep.

Thou, that sleepest the sleep of the sheep,
  And the line on thy shoulders is blue;
Were I not shy in face of the guests,
  I would run and would kiss thee asleep.

Up, hearken the owl,
  How she hoots and says;
She says: 'O Zmiḳna,
  Gone are the happy nights!'

Up, hearken the owl,
  How she hoots in the night!
She says: 'O Zmiḳna,
  Flown are the happy nights!'

Compare with this last the similar slight variations in the end of Psalm xxiv.

But such instances only remind us that Parallelism, in its many varied forms, appears in all poetries from their most primitive stage, in which it is luxuriant, to their most artistic developments. Our own folk-songs and nursery rhymes are full of it.

Over the water and over the sea,
And over the water to Charlie.

Old King Cole was a merry old soul,
And a merry old soul was he.

I love sixpence, pretty little sixpence;
I love sixpence better than my life.

They hadna sailed a league, a league,
  A league but barely three,
When the lift grew dark, and the wind blew loud,
  And gurly grew the sea.

In the more classic poetry of our language, epic, dramatic or argumentative, you will search in vain through long stretches for any instance of parallelism; and when its few occasions occur they set you thinking how far they may be due to the influence of the Old

Testament, and how, nevertheless, in spite of such influence on the most of our poets, they occur alone, and their form is not, as in Hebrew poetry, universal and dominant. Shakespeare's dramas and Milton's epics have very few. But when we turn to our native lyric and ballad poetry we find parallelism to be more prevalent, and we feel how instinctive it is in such forms. Here are some examples chosen at random:—

From Spenser's 'Epithalamion':

Open the temple gates unto my love,
Open them wide that she may enter in,
And all the posts adorn as doth behove,
And all the pillars deck with garlands trim.

From Blake:

I told my love, I told my love,
I told her all my heart.

From Burns:

Oh, open the door some pity to show,
Oh, open the door to me, oh!

From Hogg:

Lock the door, Lariston, lion of Liddesdale;
Lock the door, Lariston, Lowther comes on.

From Scott:

Why weep ye by the tide, ladye,
Why weep ye by the tide?
I'll wed ye to my youngest son,
And ye sall be his bride,
And ye sall be his bride, ladye.

Many of the songs of Burns open with a parallel couplet. And in other Scottish lyrics, and in many Irish lyrics, whether translations from the ancient Erse or modern and original, the second line is either an exact repetition of the first or only a slight variation from it.

Flow gently, sweet Afton, among thy green braes,
Flow gently, I'll sing thee a song in thy praise.

Or take this from Gray:

Ruin seize thee, ruthless King,
Confusion on thy banners wait!

Or this from 'The Ancient Mariner':[1]

Water, water everywhere,
And all the boards did shrink;
Water, water everywhere,
Nor any drop to drink!

[1] The Spirals of the Hebrew 'Songs of Degrees' find analogies in this poem. Part iii, verses 2 and 3, and in Part vii.

Or this from Campbell:

Britannia needs no bulwarks,
No towers along the steep.
Her march is on the mountain wave,
Her home is on the deep.

Much more occasionally we find it in Shelley, as in 'Queen Mab':

How wonderful is Death,
Death and his brother Sleep!

This is pure Hebrew, but it stands alone.

The following, also isolated, examples are from Tennyson's 'Lotos-eaters' and 'Maud':

Why are we weighed upon with heaviness,
And utterly consumed with sharp distress,
While all things else have rest from weariness?
All things have rest: why should we toil alone?
We only toil, who are the first of things,
And make perpetual moan,
Still from one sorrow to another thrown.

My heart would hear her and beat,
Were it earth in an earthy bed;
My dust would hear her and beat,
Had I lain for a century dead.

Or take the opening stanza of Browning's 'How they brought the Good News from Ghent to Aix'.

Or this from Meredith's 'Love in the Valley':

Shy as the squirrel and wayward as the swallow,
Swift as the swallow along the river's light.[1]

All these examples—and they might be indefinitely multiplied—appear to be original and instinctive: illustrations of a fashion natural to poetry. The fact is, poetry was primitively the art of saying the same beautiful things over and over again in similarly charming ways, which rhymed and sang back to each other not in sound only but in sense as well. 'Deep calleth unto deep,' tree to tree, bird to bird, all the world over. The heart of the poet is full of such natural antiphons. He knows many metaphors for the thing which he loves or hates, and he will put them over against each other; more careful at first that they are balanced in meaning than in rhythm, though as his art develops he will control this also to regularity. Like the musician (and the early poet always was a musician as well), he instinctively gives us variation upon variation of the same theme.

[1] I have, of course, omitted all obvious reflections of Hebrew parallelism in English hymns and other poems.

We need not, therefore, seek a Babylonian or an Egyptian origin for the parallelism of Hebrew poetry. This is due to a universal instinct, springing in all poetries and very prevalent in their earlier stages. A more difficult question is why, while the poetries of most great literatures have grown beyond the habit of parallelism, and except in their ballads and songs employ this device only occasionally, the Hebrews should have held to parallelism throughout, fostering and elaborating it with a constancy—some moderns may think with a monotony—which finds no analogy elsewhere except in parts of Babylonian poetry. It is possible that Babylonian influence had something to do with the development of parallelism in Hebrew; there is not enough evidence on the point. We saw[1] that the Arabs, though not carrying the principle so far as the Hebrews, reckoned the ability to form parallel sentences one of the highest virtues of the poet. Was this also due to Babylonian influence? We cannot tell. In any case, parallelism became the characteristic and the dominant mark of Hebrew poetry; and it is interesting to observe that of two of the commonest Hebrew verbs for the composition and singing of verses, mashal, *to rule, arrange, compare,* and 'anah, *to respond,* the first certainly, and the second probably, express this kind of verse-construction. As for the poetry of our period, whether in its ruder fragments or in its longer and more artistic pieces, we find every sort of parallelism—identical, synonymous, progressive, climactic, and antithetic. The Old Testament contains no clearer instances of all these kinds than occur in the Oracles of Balaam.

But—to return to my argument—if parallelism be the characteristic and dominant form of Hebrew verse, if the Hebrew poet be so constantly bent on a rhythm of sense, this must inevitably modify his rhythms of sound. If his first aim be to produce lines each more or less complete in itself but so as to run parallel to its fellow, it follows that these lines cannot be always exactly regular in length or in measure of time. If the governing principle of the poetry requires each line to be a clause or sentence in itself, the lines will frequently tend, of course within limits, to be longer or shorter, to have more or fewer stresses than are normal throughout the poem.

But apart from parallelism, there are other explanations of the metrical irregularities in Hebrew verse. In every form of Oriental art we trace the influence of what may be called Symmetrophobia: an instinctive aversion to absolute symmetry, which, if it knows no better, will express itself in arbitrary and even violent disturbances of the style or pattern of the work. Every visitor to the East knows

[1] Above, p. 13.

how this tendency operates, and sometimes grotesquely, in weaving and in architecture. But its opportunities are more frequent, and can be worked out more gracefully, in the art of poetry, particularly when that art is wedded to music. Professor Saintsbury has shown how numerous are the redundant syllables and the broken lines in the later blank verse of Shakespeare, and how by his hand they were made to become things of beauty: 'the irregularity was the foundation of the larger and nobler rule.'[1] 'The variation of the pause, the breaking of the line, the use of the redundant syllable, both at end and caesura, and the trisyllabic foot improved from this latter are all great things in the perfecting of the decasyllable. But, to paradox it a little, the greatest evidence of the triumph of this decasyllable is to be found in the lines which are not decasyllabic, in those which exceed and become Alexandrines, more or less regular, of which there are not a few, and in the fragments, falling short of decasyllabic length, of which there are many. For these are evidently . . . quite deliberate indulgences in excess or defect over or under a regular norm which is so pervading and so thoroughly marked that it carries them off on its wings.'[2] It is most probable that many of the metrical irregularities of the Hebrew text, exemplifying all the varieties which Professor Saintsbury enumerates in the blank verse of Shakespeare, are due to the same 'quite deliberate indulgences' on the part of the poets themselves; but it is needless to say that they are not carried off with the style of a Shakespeare. On the contrary, they are often liker the 'blundering attempts' of his predecessors in English poetry.

And, in fact, modern Arabic poetry betrays many similar irregularities. The Dutch scholar, Snouck Hurgronje, reports that in the improvisations of the singing women of Mekka 'rhyme is not exactly treated with respect, while they often push metre aside and employ the easier form of rhymed prose'.[3] In the metrical forms given in Dr. Dalman's *Palästinischer Diwan*, a collection of Arab songs taken down from the lips of the peasants and nomads of Palestine, the lines vary as much as from two to five accents, and sometimes within the same metrical form from three to four;[4] and Dr. Dalman reports that when sung to music, lines with three accents will be delivered with four, or those with four will be delivered with five to suit the melody.[5]

[1] *History of English Prosody*, vol. ii, pp. 53, 54.
[2] Ibid., p. 43.
[3] *Mekka*, vol. ii, p. 62.
[4] Cf. the Song of Deborah, where this same variation occurs.
[5] Cf. Prof. Saintsbury on the same in English poetry: 'the endeavour to match

Again, recall what has been said of the effect of the doubled consonant on Hebrew metre.[1] The licence which the poets took with regard to this may be part of the explanation of what seem to us irregularities in the time-measure of neighbouring and connected lines of verse. This conjecture is supported by the rules for the use of 'daghesh forte', the sign which duplicates a consonant. Two forms of this, 'daghesh forte dirimens' and 'daghesh forte conjunctivum', modify the vowels and syllables about them and produce a shifting of the accent. In Arabic poetry similar licence was taken with the 'teshdid', the sign analogous to the 'daghesh forte'. Now not all these signs have been preserved in our canonical text. There is some evidence from the versions that they were once more numerous in the text than they now are,[2] and it is possible that the effects which they mark—the duplication of a consonant, and the consequent increase or shifting of the accents—were frequently produced in recitation when they were not marked in the script.

With all this we must remember that we do not yet know everything about the disposition of the accents or stresses in the early poetry of Israel. We cannot say that the musical accents in our text of the poetical books adequately represent the original accentuation; and we are of course in still greater uncertainty when we deal with the accents of poetical fragments in the prose-books. In particular, there are these questions. Had each of the monosyllabic particles and conjunctions an accent to itself when placed in verse? Had the association of two nouns in the so-called 'construct state', expressive of the genitival relation, always one accent or might it have two? How often did a secondary accent occur in long nouns with the longer pronominal suffixes? The fact that modern reconstructions of the metre vary from each other and are even inconsistent with themselves in answering such questions proves how much we have still to learn about Hebrew metres.[3]

To all these considerations, then, due weight must be given before we can have assurance in emending the text of the Old Testament poems on metrical grounds *alone*; that is, by repairing what seem to our ears metrical irregularities. The zeal, manifest in many recent reconstructions of Hebrew verse, to reduce the lines to strict metre and the parallelism to absolute symmetry, seems to me, in the light of

words to music had already communicated a great apparent variety to measure.' *Op. cit.*, pp. 63, 64.

[1] Above, p. 5.

[2] For one instance see above, p. 6, on Jud. v. 22.

[3] The warning uttered by Bishop Lowth, *op. cit.*, Praelectio III, is not much less needed to-day.

what we do know about Semitic and other poetries, to be unscientific, and in the shadow of what we do not yet know to be very precarious. I cannot follow the Symmetrians.

But one fact must again be emphasized and illustrated: that a furtive vowel, whether simple or composite, never makes a syllable, and that in the reading or singing of verse it is absorbed in the next full vowel, or else the rhythm will not run. This is very evident in proper names. Take the frequent recurrence of Ya‘^{a}khobh (Jacob) in the Redes of Balaam (see Lecture III). If the lines are not to jerk badly we must read Ya‘khóbh, two syllables, the accent being on the last. Similarly with R^{e}’ubhén, and even Z^{e}bhulún and M^{e}ghiddó; and with S^{e}‘ír, ’^{E}dhóm, and ’^{A}rám and K^{e}na‘an which must be pronounced S‘īr, Dhōm, Rām, and Kná‘an. Even full vowels, I am sure, were often slurred or omitted. The name Īsra‘él (Israel) which plays so musical a part at the end of lines in the Redes of Balaam and the song of Deborah (Lecture III) may have been pronounced sometimes Sra’el or Isræl. Even in ’Is(a)skár the weight of the accent on the last syllable appears to have crushed out the preceding vowel.

A few more words may be spent on some varieties of the metre, to which allusion has been made.

One of these kinds has an interesting analogy in early European poetry. The presence of a longer, heavier line, generally at the end of a strophe,[1] is similar to what the Germans call the ‘Schwellvers’ in old German ballads. There are several instances of it in the Song of Deborah, and in the great Ode in Deuteronomy xxxii.[2] It has to be noted that the increased weight of this line is not always produced by an increase in the number of the stresses. It is sometimes due especially in couplets or triplets of a climactic parallelism to the employment of a parallel verb or noun with a greater number of syllables or with heavier consonants.[3]

In some poems the number of stresses to the line appears to remain constant (except for the ‘Schwellvers’) throughout a period or strophe, and then with a new strophe to change to another number. We shall find instances of this in the Song of Deborah, and in the opening of the Song in Deuteronomy xxxiii.[4] From such changes in the rhythm

[1] See above, p. 12.

[2] See below, Lecture III. The last two lines of verse 3 of the Song of Deborah, if we read them as one and take the construct state ‘God-of-Israel’ as under one accent; the last lines of verses 8, 10, 12, 19, and 27, and the last two of 23. In Deut. xxxii the last lines of verses 14, 24 (?), 42, 43.

[3] See below, p. 58, on Ps. xviii. 7 (8).

[4] See Lecture III.

it is not necessary to infer differences of authorship.[1] They may be due to changes in the theme.

It is also relevant to our period to say something more about the Ḳinah or elegiac measure of alternate longer and shorter lines, usually of three and two stresses each.[2] This metre reached its perfect form by the time of the great prophets, who from Amos to Jeremiah employ it with a steadily increasing frequency; and its most sustained and regular examples are found in the sixth-century Book of Lamentations, or Ḳinôth, from which it derives its modern name. But in all the poetry of our period there are very few perfect instances of the Ḳinah. There are many approximations to it, and sporadic couplets occur with its normal proportion of stresses. In other words, the Ḳinah is still rudimentary during our period, and we are able to trace its rise and development. For such couplets mainly occur in poems in which the regular rhythm is of three stresses to the line, though you also find them in series of lines of four stresses. By dropping one of these in the second line, which is easily done by omitting the dispensable verb in the second limb of the parallel or comparison, the normal Ḳinah couplet is produced. For example, the Song of Lamech,[3] in which the first two lines have four and three stresses each (if we reckon the construct state nᵉshē-Lémekh as under one accent), and the second two lines have the Ḳinah norm three and two each, the latter of these by omitting the verb.—

> ʿAdhah wᵉṢillah shᵉmaʿan ḳōlī
> Nᵉshē-Lémekh haʾᵃzīnah ʾimrathī
> Kī-ʾīsh harăghtī lᵉphiṣʿī
> Wᵉyĕlĕdh lᵉḥabbŭrathī.[4]

> ʿAdhah and Síllah, hear ye my voice,
>   Lemekh's-wives, hearken my speech,
> For a man I slew for a wound to me,
>   And a youth for a blow to me.

Or the first couplet of Lamech's other song, Genesis v. 29, the second line of which is shorter by omission of the verb.

Or the Song of the Well,[5] of which the first three lines have each

---

[1] As has been done by Carl Niebuhr in his *Versuch einer Reconstellation des Deboraliedes* (Berlin, 1894).

[2] See above, p. 12.

[3] Gen. iv. 23 ff. The rhymes guide us in the discrimination of the lines, see below, p. 24.

[4] Notice, however, that the second noun in this line is longer than that in the preceding parallel line; and may possibly have had a secondary accent in addition to the primary.

[5] Num. xxi. 17 f.

three accents, but the fourth only two, unless a secondary accent was added to the last word—

> ʿAlī bhᵉʾēr ʿᵉnū-laḥ
> Bᵉʾēr ḥᵃpharuha sarīm
> Karūha nᵉdhībhe haʿam
> Bimᵉḥoḳeḳ bᵉmishʿᵃnōtham.
>
> Spring, O Well, answer her!
> Well, princes dug her;
> Delved her folk's nobles
> With batons, with their staves.

In the opening of the Song of Moses in the Red Sea,[1] where the normal measure is two stresses to each line, the couplet—

> Yahweh ʾīsh-milḥamah
> Yahweh shᵉmo
>
> Yahweh man-of-war
> Yahweh His name—

is only possibly a Ḳinah couplet; the construct state in the first line may be under one stress.

In the Oracles of Balaam, in which the usual number of accents to the line is three, there are several couplets with four-three and with three-two.[2] In the Song of Deborah, in which some divisions have two accents to the line and others three, and a few four, we find only three couplets in the Ḳinah proportion of three to two.[3] In the Blessing of the Tribes in Genesis xlix, in which the normal measure is three stresses to each line, it is possible to read rough couplets of the Ḳinah in verses 11, 13, 14, 17; while in its counterpart, Deuteronomy xxxiii, both couplets of verse 3, both of 10, one in 9, and those in 18 and 25 are regular Ḳinah couplets. The Song in Deuteronomy xxxii affords by far the largest number of actual instances of the Ḳinah rhythm,[4] but it is instructive that on other grounds this poem has been reckoned to be later than our period. The 'Mashal' on Saul and David, quoted thrice in the First Book of Samuel,[5] is a genuine Ḳinah couplet produced by the means mentioned above, the omission of the verb in the second parallel clause.

> Hikkah Shaʾūl baʾᵃlaphau
> Wᵉdhawīdh bᵉribhᵉbhothau
>
> Slain hath Shaʾūl his thousands
> But David his myriads.

[1] Exod. xv. 3.

[2] For example, Numbers xxiii. 9 (1st and possibly 2nd couplet), 10 (2nd c.), 24, xxiv. 5, 7, 18c–19a.

[3] Judges v. 1, 6, and perhaps the first of 19. See Lecture III.

[4] e. g. verses 11, 14, 16, 21, 23 (?), 24 f., 29, 30–2, 34, 36, 39, 41.

[5] xviii. 7, xxi. 12, xxix. 5.

In David's Dirge on Saul and Jonathan,[1] in which we might have expected the Ḳinah or elegiac measure throughout (had this been by that time perfected), there are only three, or possibly four, instances of it.[2] In the three couplets of the Dirge on Abner,[3] the last two may fairly be reckoned as of this elegiac measure, but they are irregular.

This survey confirms the statement, with which I started this section of the lecture, that in the earlier poetry of Israel the Ḳinah rhythm is still rudimentary. It has not reached the consummate form in which it appears from the eighth century onwards.

Once more—though this be a digression from our period—something must be said about the rhythm of the discourses of the great prophets. It is generally agreed that portions of these were composed and delivered as metrically as any of the Psalms. But the text shows many irregularities, and the poetry is often broken by what is sheer prose. The Versions help us to remove some of the former; while much of the prose proves itself to be a later insertion by its interruption or even contradiction of the metrical verses with which it is entangled; or by its very weakness and banality. But at the same time, considering the rhetorical purpose of the prophets, we should expect to find in their discourses an even greater liberty in the metrical forms which they employ; and it is not surprising that sometimes they pass over to prose. Consider what was said above of the Mekkan improvisations. With regard to irregularities in the prophetic metre, the following sentence on the speeches of the Elizabethan drama is not irrelevant: 'When Dr. Johnson reprehended, in a famous phrase, the mixing of the methods of the poet and the declaimer, he was unconsciously describing the real virtue of the thing—the application, as no other poetic form has ever mastered it, of the double appeal of poetry and rhetoric, the magical order of poetry, and the magical *apparent* freedom of rhetoric.'[4]

In conclusion, some words on Alliteration, Assonance, and Rhyme.

Some alliteration and some assonance are inevitable consequences from the prevailing parallelism, but in this case they frequently, of course, consist in the repetition of the same words. In the passages quoted above from the Psalms and from Isaiah to illustrate the music

[1] 2 Sam. i. 19 ff.

[2] Verses 21 (?), 25, 26. See Lecture III.

[3] 2 Sam. iii. 33, 34.

[4] Saintsbury, *op. cit.*, pp. 21, 22. Snouck Hurgronje reports that in the same Molid—a kind of Memorabilia of the Prophet recited at Mekka—poems and rhymed prose usually succeed each other (*Mekka*, ii. p. 147).

derived from a mingling of the liquids and softer radicals, and from the use of the doubled consonant, and from the attempts to echo the booming and crashing of the sea, we have examples of the expertness in the art of Assonance possessed by the later poets of Israel.

In the poetry of our period this art is not so well developed or sustained; but words containing the same or similar letters, though it be only one of each, are often placed in immediate succession to each other, or are grouped in the same couplet, so that little rills of music are let loose; yet they never run far.[1] Alliteration, apart from the repetition of the same word in the parallelism, is infrequent.[2]

Nor is Rhyme usual in the longer poems; but it occurs in not a few of the shorter pieces, and the same rhyme is carried through all their lines as in some Arab forms, or, as in other Arab forms, through all save the last two or three lines. Take the Song of Lamech[3]—

> ʿAdhah w^{e}Ṣillah sh^{e}maʿan ḳōlī
> N^{e}shē-Lémekh ha'^{a}zīnah 'imrathī
> Kī 'īsh haraghtī l^{e}phiṣʿī
> W^{e}yeledh l^{e}ḥabburathī.
>
> Adah and Ṣillah, hear ye the voice of me,
> Lemekh's-wives, hearken the speech of me,
> For a man have I slain for a wound to me,
> And a youth for a blow to me.

The next and concluding couplet does not rhyme.

Or take the second fragment attributed to Lamech, the subject of which is Noah's introduction, or revival, of the culture of the vine[4]—

> Zĕh y^{e}naḥ^{a}mēnū mimmaʿ^{a}sēnū
> Ūmeʿiṣ^{e}bhōn yadhēnū
> [Min ha'^{a}dhamah '^{a}shĕr 'er^{e}raḥ Yahweh].
>
> This doth relieve us from the work of us,
> From the toil of the hands of us,
> [Out of the ground the which Yahweh cursed].

Here again the rhyme fails in the last line—if indeed the last line be genuine.

Or take the Philistine taunt of Samson[5]—

> Nathan '^{e}lōhēnū bh^{e}yadhēnū 'eth-'oy^{e}bhēnū
> W^{e}'eth-maḥ^{a}rībh 'arṣēnū
> Wa'^{a}shĕr hirbah 'eth-h^{a}lalēnū.

[1] One of the most evident is the use of the sibilants in the Song of Lamech. There are several in the Oracles of Balaam, and others in 2 Sam. i. 21, 22, 23.

[2] Gen. xxvii. 27; Judges v. 4, 18; xiv. 14, 18.

[3] Gen. iv. 23. [4] Gen. v. 29. [5] Judges xvi. 24.

Gave the god of us, to the hands of us, the foe of us,
And the waster of the lands of us,
Who multiplied the slain of us.

One other example, the women's eulogy of David[1]—

Hikkah Sha'ūl ba'^{a}laphau
W^{e}dhawidh b^{e}ribh^{e}bhothau.

Slain hath Sha'ūl the thousands of him,
But David the myriads of him.

An analysis of all the poems and poetical fragments of our period shows that there are about twelve with no rhymed couplets, and that in all the others there are about forty-five rhymed couplets. Of these no fewer than twenty-eight rhyme, like the instances quoted above, on the same pronominal suffixes; two on plurals in -īm, and four on proper names terminating in the same syllable (for example, -ōn). The lines of four or five other couplets conclude with synonymous names, divine or human.

What is true of the poems of our period is true of Old Testament poetry throughout. The vast majority of the rhymes which are found in it are formed by the recurrence of the same pronominal suffixes—the suffixes which in Hebrew are equivalent to our personal pronouns. Occasionally rhymes are formed on the plural terminations -īm or -ōth, and more rarely on the plural termination of the verb, -ûn. But it is significant, that we often find that the lines of the poems terminate in names at once musical and famous: like Isra'el or Yeshurun, or one or other of the names of the Deity. And still more significant is the postponement to the ends of the lines of synonymous verbs or nouns which do not rhyme. This is but another proof that to the taste of early (as of later) Israel it was more natural to produce a parallel (or antithesis) of meaning than a harmony of sound.

Finally there are a few instances of Paronomasia, or play upon words: as for example Genesis, v. 29 on the name of Noah, ix. 27 on the name of Japheth, xlix. 16 on that of Dan, 19 on Gad, and Deuteronomy xxxiii. 8 on Meribhah. Perhaps also in the couplet, in Judges v. 12, a similar echo is intended between the name Deborah in the first line and the verb dabberu in the second.

[1] I Sam. xviii. 7.

LECTURE II

SUBSTANCE AND SPIRIT.

ALTHOUGH the inspiration of the greatest minds in Israel was something unique in the ancient East, and although (as we shall see) a certain distinction between the people and all their neighbours may be traced even in that early period of their history with which we are dealing; nevertheless Israel was no isolated creation. The qualities, which equipped the people for their spiritual service to humanity, were their natural inheritance as children of that family of mankind to whom we give the ambiguous name of Semites, but whose common genius for religion, common religious institutions, common powers and forms of prophecy, missionary zeal and capacity for martyrdom have proved in history to be anything but ambiguous. And so in particular with Hebrew poetry. Neither its spirit, nor the aspects of nature nor the human interests with which it is occupied, nor its characteristic forms can be adequately appreciated, except by comparison with, and frequent illustration from, the poetries of those other Semitic tribes with whom Israel shared the same blood,[1] the same or similar physical conditions, the same forms of language, the same economy, and in part the same historical experiences.

It is a question whether Arabia was the cradle of the Semitic race; but no one doubts that upon this vast peninsula and the deserts intruding from it upon Syria—the deserts from which Israel themselves came up—the racial type has been most faithfully preserved from the earliest times to the present day. Upon Arabia nature has bestowed few gifts beyond that of breeding men. A ribbon of fertility round most of the coast line, and broadening considerably on the Indian Ocean, encloses a high, bare and broken plateau, with stretches of absolutely barren rock and shifting sand; but also with wider regions from which the annual rains entice a sparse and quickly withered vegetation; while at the roots of hills where springs rise, or in the hollows where underground waters gather and can be tapped, there are oases of real fertility. The life of man is mainly pastoral, with a comparatively small proportion of agriculture and very few industries. The popula-

[1] It is possible that this prevailing Semitic strain of Israel was crossed by non-Semitic strains, e.g. the Hittite, but that is a question which cannot be discussed here.

tion is broken up into tribes, that are defined not by the more or less vague areas over which they roam in search of pasture, but by ties of blood and kinship, supplemented by fictions of a common descent or other artificial expedients. Famine and war are the annual curses of their life. The insufficiency of water and pasture; the strain of hunger and the jealousy of blood, all the heat and recklessness which are bred of poverty and pride; the constant temptations to raid the camels and cattle of other tribes; with the sacred obligation which binds a whole tribe to avenge the slaughter of one of its members—all these create a climate of feud; while the necessity of living in shifting camps, and the absence (except for rare moments in the history) of economic or military interests common to the whole peninsula, and of an authority effective over so vast and wild a surface, render impossible any polity save of the most loose and friable kind. Such incoherence, derived from residence in these deserts perhaps for millennia before the race broke into history, has cursed to the end even the most settled and progressive of Semitic peoples. Israel itself is an illustration.

Within the tribe order and authority have always been more or less vague. There is, of course, unwritten, consuetudinary law; but behind it little executive force. The tribal sheikh or 'senior' is but *primus inter pares*; and in the camp, devoid of gaols [1] or police, he has nothing to enforce his decisions, or those of the tribal judge, or those of the 'kāhin', the representative of the deity and therefore the final court of appeal, except his personal influence and the power of public opinion. In such a society the strongest moral motive is shame—shame before one's parents or before one's fellow-tribesmen, and this is reflected in what Wellhausen calls the only moral name for God among the Arabs before the rise of Islam, el-Wasi, the Restrainer. In such an ethical temper the importance of certain forms of poetry is obvious. In a sense more exact and acute than the author of the phrase has used it, poetry becomes 'the criticism of life'. Its eulogies and satires focus public opinion and enforce the unwritten law of the desert more keenly than the sword itself. Very frequent, both in early Israel and among the Arabs, are the songs which praise the brave, the liberal and the true, or taunt the coward, the niggardly and the treacherous.

The vendetta or system of blood-revenge by which the duty of punishing a murderer is imposed, not on some executive authority but on the whole family or clan whose blood he has outraged, has been

[1] Thieves and other defaulters are bound to the ropes of the sheikh's tent and subjected to torture. Musil, *Arabia Petraea, iii, Ethnologischer Reisebericht.*

called the 'one element of jurisprudence in the wild life of the desert'. It springs from the simple principle of blood for blood—

Who sheds the blood of man
By man his blood be shed—[1]

of one life for one life. But the nomads have formally developed this to a degree of which the practical consequences are incalculable. Should the murderer himself escape, his punishment may be exacted of any of his kinsmen to the fifth generation; if none of these are within reach, every ally or client of his tribe, nay even every person from the same district or nation, is in peril of being slain in his stead. The moral effects of such a system are twofold and contrary. On the one hand it undoubtedly restrains from murder. The infinite possibilities of vengeance which it lets loose engender a reluctance to take life except in self-defence—a reluctance which all travellers in Arabia have observed with surprise even among the wildest tribes. But on the other hand when once a man has been slain, the excitement of whole tribes to the punishment of the deed becomes a fertile source of disorder, of injustice—as in the case of accidental manslaughter—and of tribal war, which may last, and has lasted, for a century at a time. The right to slay is not confined to open war; under it all kinds of crafty assassination occur, and even when they are accomplished in violation of other rights, like the sacred one of hospitality, they are praised—as in the case of Jael and Sisera—in the name of religion. Beneath such widespread and enduring responsibilities—on the one side for the guilt and on the other for the expiation of the murder—no man on meeting a stranger can tell how he stands to him, and fear and mistrust prevail. Wherever a central authority has been established among the nomads one of its first attempts has been either to mitigate the excesses of the system or to do away with it altogether.[2]

More certain are the moral benefits of that traditional right of sanctuary by which the violence of the vendetta is mitigated. Even to the guiltiest who crave it, asylum is granted in every tent in Arabia; and the respite may be used for the investigation of the case, or for some compromise between the slayer and the relations of the slain.

So much for the tribe. There never was a nation in Arabia till

[1] Gen. ix. 6. See below, Lecture III, p. 46 *n.* 3.

[2] See Robertson Smith, *Religion of the Semites*, and Doughty, *Arabia Deserta* (both *passim*), for the theory and practice respectively of the system. But one of the best accounts of it I know is given in Von Oppenheim's *Vom Mittelmeer zum Persischen Golf*, ii. 92–4. To all of these I am indebted for the above details. The last gives several instances of attempts to put down the system by the Wahabees, Mohammed 'Ali, the Russians in the Caucasus, and the Sublime Porte.

Mohammed fused the tribes for a time by the fierce heat of his religion and the passion for spoil. But occasionally trade has thrown round these jealous and restless groups of men a long and a strong bond. The oases form islands in the sea of the desert; and the eminent fertility of the southern coast, with its conspicuous product of incense, so sacred a requisite of the ancient civilisations at the other end of the peninsula, developed from oasis to oasis a considerable commerce, and turned the nomadic tribes who possessed camels (at first unknown to those civilisations) into confederacies of carriers. The southern kingdom of Sheba or Saba was built on commerce. Mekka, on the main line of traffic thence to Syria and Egypt, was a great market as well as a shrine. Mohammed himself, before he became a prophet, led a trading caravan from Mekka to Damascus, the great harbour of civilisation on the northern coast of the desert. You will remember that one of the earliest[1] appearances of Arabs in the Old Testament is as traders: Ishmaelites or Midianites carrying spices and frankincense into Egypt.

The restlessness of the Semite was not confined to his vast breeding ground. Fertile mother but poor nurse of men, Arabia has ever urged her hungry children upon the rich lands to the north and the west of her—Babylonia, Syria and Egypt. The history of her frontiers is a history of migrations: heavy tides of men which in time burst even the strongest bulwarks opposed to them, and rush, or soak and trickle, into full possession of the civilisations beyond. By ways both of peace and war, often against their will and in despite of their desert pride, the nomads are drawn into the beginnings of agriculture. Sometimes they delay the economic change, which they dread, and content themselves with imposing blackmail on the peasants or employing these as serfs for their planting and reaping. *The sons of the alien are their ploughmen and vinedressers.* But the end is inevitable. They grow discontented with the pits in which they store their grain. They build barns and walls about their orchards, with, in time, towers to protect these and the wells which they have appropriated. They go into caves or stone houses for the winter, but ultimately they abandon their tents even in summer and build stone or clay houses for occupation all the year round. In the course of four or five journeys along the desert frontiers of Syria I have seen every stage of this long transition from the nomad and pastoral forms of life to the settled and agricultural: a process infinitely more gradual and complex than that academic division into nomadic and semi-nomadic, into fellahin and half-fellahin which is the fashion

[1] Gen. xxxvii. 25-8.

with some writers at the present day.[1] Nor after their final settlement to agriculture do such immigrants soon grow away from their tribal constitution or relinquish their tribal customs. They do not readily combine into nations, and the nations frequently break up again. They continue to practise the vendetta, modified by the rights of sanctuary, and preserve many other institutions derived from their nomadic ancestors. There is no fuller illustration of all this than the history of Israel.

Such a society—desert-born and desert-bred, but in its more vigorous elements migrating to the fertile lands and adventuring on the economic changes which this involves—determined the human themes of the poetry of the race. Besides love and war, courage and death, these themes are the following: the pastoral life with its providence for the beasts and its benevolence to strangers; not patriotism nor civic pride as with ourselves, but pride of blood and family; famous genealogies, tribal origins and histories; tribal loyalties, hospitalities and powers of vengeance; or migration and travel; the long desert journeys; the shiftings of the camps; the desolate aspects of abandoned sites, the hollow hearths with their cold ashes, the rows of stones marking where the fringes of the black tents have touched the ground—a scene so familiar and so moving to the Arab that certain classic forms of his poetry, whatever be their main subject, invariably start with the description of this. Some further remarks are necessary.

First, in Arabia before the times of Islam women as well as men were poets, and you can understand how the more proper themes of their verse were the return of their victorious warriors to the camp; the lamentation of the dead, dirges being mainly (though not exclusively) the office of women; and things deserving of satire and taunts, feminine powers in this line being recognized among the Semites as everywhere else.[2] Women were frequently spectators of the tribal battles, and since they were more free than the fighters to see the whole action and more able to award praise and blame, it does not surprise us to find from women some of the most vivid ballads of war. This also appears in the early poetry of Israel.

Secondly, the songs of travel say wonderfully little of trade. Trade appears to have inspired or influenced the poetry of the Semites as slightly as it did their religion.[3] There are, of course, scattered meta-

[1] See further the author's *Jerusalem: its Topography, Economics and History*, i. 285 ff.; *Expositor*, Seventh Series, No. 33, p. 254 ff.

[2] On Satire see below, pp. 37, 38.

[3] See *Encyclopaedia Biblica*, 'Trade and Commerce' (by the present writer), §§ 21–24.

phors suggested by commerce; like that fine figure in which the disburdening of the clouds, come up from the sea and hanging low on the horizon, is likened to the loosening and emptying of a merchant's bales on the floor of the market.[1]

Thirdly, some of the classic metres of Arab poetry are derived by experts from the rhythmic movements of the camel or horse on the long desert journeys. This should have been noticed in last lecture. The beat of horses' hoofs is metrically rendered in one of the couplets of the Song of Deborah.

And again, the panoramas of desert scenery which the songs of travel unroll are lists of place-names, but each name is skilfully woven into the music and has a small vivid picture attached to it; so that these songs are among the most stirring pieces of Arab poetry.[2]

The natural phenomena of the desert are few and simple. Far from the sea coast with its perpetual strife of land and water, and far from the river deltas with their visible creation of land out of water, the Arabian nomads know nothing of those materials of the great cosmogonies, developed by Semites who left Arabia and settled in Mesopotamia or on the Delta of Egypt or on the Syrian coast. Nor is there in the desert any rush of vegetation with the spring, nor apart from the Dead Sea Valley has there been within human memory a living volcano—in short no suggestions of forces that could make or ruin worlds. The nomad lies between the bare stones and the clear stars. The only physical processes which excite his imagination are the dawn and the sunset, the passage of the planets, the shadows flung by great rocks, the rustle of the desert breeze, the mysterious crackle and whisper of the earth's surface when the night cold grips it; the rain and the thunderstorm. Thus any mythology which arose in Arabia was virtually exhausted in the identification of the gods with sun, moon and stars above and with the rocks below, whether these were the great cliffs that cast a beneficent shadow or were meteoric stones fallen from heaven and worshipped as images of deity; and in the recognition of theophanies and divine actions in the thunderstorm and rainbow—two favourite themes of Arab poets. Every traveller on the desert is familiar with the mysterious crackling which rises into the still air on the fall of a cold night. It is this which probably suggested the belief so prevalent among the Semites that the dry places of the desert—as distinguished from those regions of the earth which a god has manifestly endowed for himself with water and fertility—are thronged by jinns and demons innumerable, which,

[1] See below, Lecture III, p. 60.

[2] For an example see below, Lecture III, p. 59; cf. 62, 63.

however, invade from there the houses and persons of the inhabitants of settled lands. A curious trace of this imagination occurs in the parable of our Lord where the unclean spirit driven out of a man walked through *dry places* seeking rest and returned to the house from whence he came out.[1] Musil tells us that the Ṣkhûr, the great Arab tribe on the eastern border of Moab, 'hear at night in the desert all sorts of voices, al-mfâyel'; and that 'female spirits, ad-daffafiyât, appear in the desert every night from Thursday to Friday, playing on tambourines, ad-dfûf, beating drums, at-tbûl, and dancing to them. No one dare approach these, else he must dance with them till he falls down dead'.[2] And again 'in the desert one must not whistle, for whoso whistles calls the devils together, therefore every Ṣakhari gets angry with whistling and bids the whistler cease'.[3] I once asked one of my servants, not a Bedawee but a city-bred Syrian, to draw some water for me after dark from a cistern in the desert of Judaea. He excused himself, and when I insisted he trembled. When I said, 'What do you fear? You will see nothing there,' he replied: 'It is not what I shall see, but what I cannot see, that I fear.' I know what he was thinking: that the unseen spirits might crowd and hustle him into the water, as he bent over it to draw.

When the nomad left the desert for some oasis or the margin of the fertile lands, his first emotions were roused by fountains and trees. Contrasted with his stagnant cisterns, often covered by a green scum, the fountains were to him alive—he called them living water. The sudden and voluminous outbreaks of water, often as fullgrown streams, which happen between the harder and softer strata of the Syrian limestones, appeared to be the work of some underground god. As I have said elsewhere, no one may imagine how possessed such a landscape feels, as if chosen, overpowered, married and fertilised by some deity—Be'ulah the Hebrews called it, Ba'al's land the Arabs—who has not across the forsaken plateaus to the east of Moab or on the desert flanks of Anti-Lebanon fallen on one of the sudden Syrian rivers with its wealth of verdure. No wonder that we find songs addressed to the wells as if they were living beings and of divine power. Nilus describes Arabs about a well in the desert 'singing hymns' to it.[4]

Again, there are the trees—singly or in scattered groves—to which in his bare silent deserts the Arab was unaccustomed. Taking his

1 Matt. xii. 43 f.; Luke xi. 24.
2 *Arabia Petraea, iii, Ethnologischer Reisebericht*, 323.
3 Ibid. 313.
4 Migne, *Patrologiae, Patres Graeci*, Ser. I, Tom. 79, Sp. 648.

mid-day rest beneath them in the stillness of that hour in the east, the nomad might fall asleep with only gratitude in his heart for the shade they flung over him. But in the cool of the day he would waken with their rustling before the breeze, and startled by the voice of God, put up his prayers before he passed on. I have felt it myself on my return to the neighbourhood of trees after only a fortnight in the desert stillness.

From the social and physical influences upon the poetry of the race I pass to its personal sources in the racial temperament and genius. Like human nature everywhere the nature of the Semite is a bundle of paradoxes; but his particular paradoxes are explained by the discipline of the desert, endured—I must repeat for the point is essential—endured perhaps for millennia before the race broke into history.

The first of these paradoxes is the combination of strong sensual grossness with equally strong tempers of reverence and worship. Mr. Doughty has most emphasized this, but it is obvious throughout the race. He somewhat violently likens the Arab to a man sitting in a cloaca up to the eyes but his brows touch heaven. The Arab is a shepherd and cattle-breeder, his own butcher, and lying at nights with his beasts about him. But the long fasts, which he annually endures, purge the body and lend to the mind a swift detachment from the things of sense.[1] We find one type of this double temper in Jacob the father of the tribes of his people: a hardy, unscrupulous herdsman, yet capable of spiritual dreams and of wrestling with the unseen. We shall see another in Balaam and in his counterpart Mohammed.[2]

The second paradox is a marvellous capacity for endurance and resignation broken by fits of ferocity: the ragged patience usually bred by famine. We see it survive in the long-suffering, mingled with outbursts of implacable wrath, which characterizes so many Psalms. These are due to long periods of moral famine, the famine of justice, from which such Psalms are to be dated.

The third paradox, equally explicable by the life of the desert, is a versatile subtilty of mind, devoid both of originality in thinking and of the power of sustained argument and imagination.[3]

And the fourth is a distinct subjectiveness in the Semite's attitude to the phenomena of nature and of history, combined with as distinct an objectiveness or realism in describing these phenomena.

[1] *Arabia Deserta*, i, pp. 56, 400, 467, 473; ii. 336, 378.
[2] Lecture III, p. 69.
[3] See above, Introd. and Lecture I, p. 10.

These last two I take together in their influence on the poetry of the race.

The detachableness of mind from the things of sense, of which I have just spoken as one effect of the influence of the desert, is prevented by the stern necessities of the nomad life from becoming mere visionariness or speculation. To the nomad on his bare, war-swept soil few things happen, but everything that happens is ominous; as Amos, himself a shepherd of the desert, has illustrated.[1] It has not come there without some intention towards, some meaning for, the observer himself or his tribe. Hence the temper of Semitic feeling and reflection is as different from the contemplative repose of the sages of the further East, as it is from those sustained and intricate powers of argument which have grown upon the western mind in the security and leisure of the great civilisations. The leisure of the desert is vast, but it is the leisure of the sentinel: of a man required to observe and reason, yet his reasoning, till he settles and becomes subject to civilisation on some sea-coast or river-delta, is not roused to the first causes of things; nor, except under the influence of a religion like Israel's, does his imagination travel forth to their ultimate destiny. He is engrossed with their impression on himself for the moment, their significance for his tribe and their effect on its present situation. The Semitic nomad's interest in phenomena is practical, and its practical nature persists even after his settlement in civilisation: as we see in the case of Israel and their religion. For that religion continued to be largely engrossed with the bearing of the facts of nature and history upon the fortunes of Israel themselves; and it required all the ethical powers of prophecy to control and purify so self-regarding a temper. To the last the Hebrew mind is not speculative, except when crossed by foreign influences, as it is at one end of the history in the makers of the cosmogonies, and as at the other, for example, in Spinoza.

This sentinel attitude of the mind has set the temper of Semitic poetry. To it are due the opposite qualities of that poetry—opposite but equally great. We constantly hear Semitic poetry called 'subjective'. So it is if by 'subjective' is meant self-regarding, and to this I shall return.[2] But at the same time it is thoroughly realistic, regarding things not under a leisurely and reflective fancy but as the practical observer feels the impression of them at the moment of their appearance. Hence the prevailingly lyric form of the poetry and its simple, concrete and lucid character. Bishop Lowth does not exaggerate when he says that Hebrew

[1] Amos iii. 3-8. [2] See below, pp. 36, 37.

verse illustrates and exemplifies the remark of Aristotle [1] that 'the great excellence of the poetic dialect consists in perspicuity without meanness'. Even in order to express the mysterious or to attain the sublime the Semite never resorted to the vague or the obscure. This is true of Arabic poetry, when untouched by Persian mysticism, and it is equally true of the poetry of the Hebrews with their deeper sense of the mystery of life and their grander conceptions of God. In this we may contrast the Semite with the Celt. They are at extremes both geographically and in the matter of climate; but not more different are the mists which roll round Ireland and the Hebrides from the shadowless landscapes of Arabia than the obscurity and vagueness of the sublime in Celtic poetry is from its sharp outline and clear shining in the poetry of the Semites. The cause is not only the physical atmosphere in which all great things stand out simple and clear. It is also that habit of mind which is bred in the nomad by the necessity of forming rapid and sharp conceptions of all phenomena.[2]

The accuracy of the poetry in its description of nature is matched by its truthfulness in recording events. In this the Arab poet shows a conscience. There is a couplet by Zuhair, which Sir Charles Lyall has fitly adopted as the motto of his admirable translations of ancient Arab poems—

'Of all the verses which thou hast made the fairest to praise
Is that whereof, when they hear, men say, Yes, that is the truth!'

In this we have, as every modern authority insists, the warrant of the historical value of the poetry. The Arabs themselves emphasized it. They call their poetry 'the public register of the Arab people; by its means genealogies are remembered, and glorious deeds handed down to posterity'; and Muḥammed ibn Salem el-Jumahi says: 'Verse in the days of the Ignorance was to the Arabs the Register of all they knew and the utmost compass of their wisdom; with it they began their affairs and with it they ended them.' [3] Herr Musil records the extraordinary powers of two Arab herd-boys, to whom he listened at the Kalʿat el-Ḥsa, as they sang the genealogies and great deeds of their own and other tribes.[4]

[1] *Poet.* 22.

[2] Since writing the above paragraph I have come across the following remarks on the Arab poets by Wellhausen (*Cosmopolis*, Feb. 1896, p. 598): 'Sie phantasieren nicht ins Blaue hinein, sondern halten sich streng an die Wirklichkeit, weil sie nicht anders können, weil sie in der genauesten Beobachtung lebendiger und unlebendiger Wesen aufgewachsen sind. Diese Poesie klebt am Boden und ist im höchsten Grade realistisch.'

[3] Both quoted by Sir Charles Lyall: *Ancient Arabian Poetry*, p. xv.

[4] *Arabia Petraea, Moab*, p. 84.

We can appreciate, however, the serious damage to which the historical value of such poetry was exposed by the oral tradition on which its survival so long depended. Faults of ear, memory and temper were inevitable as it was repeated from one tribe, or one generation, to another. Different singers would have different favourites among its heroes; and as it passed across Arabia different tribal prejudices would play upon it. Thus errors, confusions and even deliberate alterations were multiplied. Just as in Hebrew, two or more editions of the same poem became current. Fragments originally distinct were pieced together. Or the author of a poem was forgotten and his work attributed to another.

We must remember, too, the other side of the paradox. So realist a poetry is preserved from becoming the mere enumeration of things seen, only by the acute interest or fervent passion which the poet's own experience of them has excited. The Semite has not a distant imagination. No literatures suffer more than his from separation in space or time between the writer and his subject. It is true that the Old Testament holds much great poetry, both in prose and verse, which appears to prove the contrary. How vividly, for instance, have the Deuteronomists of the eighth or seventh centuries repainted in their own rich style the distant wanderings in the wilderness, or the late poet of Deuteronomy xxxii rendered the passage of Israel from the desert to the fertile land! But that is due first to their extraordinarily vivid religion, their burning sense of God and His way through the ages, and, secondly, to the passion with which the individual Israelite threw himself into the personality of his Mother the Nation and felt again, as though they were his own, her secular sufferings and sins. On the other hand, even in the Old Testament, history at a distance is the mere inflation of older annals by exaggeration of their statements and moralising additions to the events they record. Contrast the contemporary or nearly contemporary narratives of David in the Books of Samuel with the account of his reign in Chronicles. Some of the later Psalms, which rehearse the history of Israel, are little more than lists of events and names which even their warm piety does not always redeem from stiffness and a stale savour. With regard to journeys, adventures, battles, mournings and the like, in order to be effective a writer of the Semitic class of imagination must have been in living touch with what he describes. Wellhausen[1] has remarked how much of the

[1] *Cosmopolis*, Feb. 1896, p. 599: 'Vielfach fällt Dichter und Held zusammen. . . . Wenn aber ein berufsmässiger Dichter von den Taten Anderer singt, so sind es die Taten eines lebenden Helden, dem er nahe steht, oder es sind die Taten seines Stammes, die so gut wie seine eigenen sind.'

best Arab poetry before Mohammed was written by men or women who were either actors in the scenes they celebrated or closely associated with these. The bearing of this on those early poems of Israel which are attributed to the leaders of the actions they vividly describe, Moses, Miriam or Deborah, is obvious; and I shall return to it in the next lecture.

The same personal interest of the authors in their subjects led them to mix with their descriptions a great deal of another kind of poetry. 'The Arabian ode sets before us a series of pictures drawn with confident skill and first-hand knowledge of the life its maker lived, of the objects among which he moved, of his horse, his camel, the wild creatures of the wilderness, and of the landscape in the midst of which his life and theirs was set; but all, however loosely they seem to be bound together, are subordinate to one dominant idea which is the poet's unfolding of himself, his admirations and his hates, his prowess and the freedom of his spirit.'[1] Of this testimony an emphatic corroboration is given by Dr. Georg Jacob in his *Altarabisches Beduinenleben*[2]: 'Das beschreibende Element ist stark in der altarabischen Poesie vertreten, dem entspricht auch die durchweg stichische Komposition der Gedichte, aber es ist keine objektive epische Beschreibung, sondern eine unruhige skizzenhafte, untrennbar verwoben mit dem Ich, der stark ausgeprägten Subjektivität des Dichters.' Hence the readiness with which the realist narrative poetry of the Arabs passes into that of a very subjective 'criticism of life': a criticism inspired by personal or tribal interests and passions.[3] Their poems of war abound in praise and blame. Satire especially is frequent: taunt-songs whether upon the foe or upon the indolent and cowardly of the poet's own tribe; and delivered both as incitements on the onset to the battle or at its close in the poetry both of triumph and lamentation. This form of poem, the Higā', was probably developed, as Goldziher[4] has shown, from the solemn curses which poets were called in to pronounce upon the enemy as the tribe went out to meet him; and which, as inspired, were believed to be as essential to victory as the arms and the courage of the tribe. 'You are a poet, help us with your tongue,' cried a warrior of the Ḳureish to a singer before the battle of Bedr.[5] Of the same kind

[1] *Op. cit.*, xviii. [2] p. 202. [3] Lyall, *loc. cit.*

[4] *Abhandlungen zur arabischen Philologie*, Erster Theil (1896), pp. 1-121.

[5] Mr. Nicholson in his *Literary History of the Arabs*, p. 124, quotes from the *Kitab-el-'Aghani* a story of the poet el-A'shá, who on his way to recite to Mohammed a poem in his honour was intercepted by the Ḳoreish and bribed to be silent. 'O ye Ḳoreish,' cried Abu Sufyán, 'this is A'shá, and, by God, if he becomes a follower of Mohammed he will inflame the Arabs against you by his poetry. Collect, therefore, a hundred camels for him.'

was the spell which Balaķ of Moab called Balaam to pronounce upon Israel. And of the other kind of satire, delivered after the battle both upon allies and enemies, we have rich instances in the Song of Deborah; but notice that the prophetess had also been called to deliver a song *before* the battle.[1]

Another consequence of the 'subjective', passionate temper of Arabic poetry is the well-known absence from it of the epic. Lyrics, ballads, odes, besides metrical proverbs and riddles—all these we find, but no epic. Its place is taken, as has been frequently said, by the Prose-romance, combined of personal narrative, family tradition and myth, frequently quoting older verse or breaking out into verse of its author's own making.

One other general feature of early Arabic poetry must be mentioned, and most fitly here, for it is partly due to the realism of the nomad, and his absorption in the present situation. Arabic poetry is almost entirely devoid of hope or imagination of a life beyond the grave. The few sparks of these, which are struck in Arabia before Mohammed, have been reasonably attributed to the impact of Jewish or Christian ideas on the Arab mind. Now the nomads are not without belief in the continued existence of their dead. When passing recent graves in the sand I have heard my Bedawee guides call on the buried by name, and have sometimes observed them pour on the ground a little of our drinking-water as if for their refreshment. Arabs also make pilgrimages to the tombs of famous ancestors and sacrifice to them.[2] It nevertheless remains true, that they have no clear conceptions of a life hereafter, with or without God, or of a resurrection or of a judgement. Travellers among them have remarked on the wonder of this, after twelve centuries of the teaching of Islam on such subjects. The reason, as I have remarked, is in part the absorption of the nomad's mind by the stress and strain of his present life; and in part the fact that the tribal interests, the security and the survival of the tribe in this life, overwhelm the individual's interests, and the importance of what may happen to him hereafter. But perhaps also the nomadic form of life is part of the explanation. The living do not continually dwell beside their people's graves, and these disappear and are forgotten. There are no solid sepulchres, and very few inscribed monuments.[3] It takes a settled community, living beside their dead, and kept in remembrance by stable and eloquent monuments, to habituate the imagination to the subject of

[1] Judges v. 12. See below, Lecture III.

[2] Musil, *Arabia Petraea, iii, Ethnologischer Reisebericht,* 329 ff.

[3] Doughty, i. 241, 618, &c.

their fate and to develop dogmas and pictures of the life to come; as we see in the case of the Semites' neighbours the Egyptians, and also among Semites who left the nomadic life and settled in Babylonia to the inheritance of an older civilisation. In spite of their desert traditions these also achieved strong and detailed conceptions of the world of the dead; but this was always done under the figures of the dusty, bat-haunted tombs which they learned to build and carve in proximity to their own homes.

During this survey of the character of the primitive Semites and of the circumstance and main directions of their life, I have noticed some illustrations of the subject in the early history and poetry of Israel. But these illustrations by no means exhaust the parallel between the circumstance and experience of Israel and those of her Semitic kinsmen; nor the consequent resemblances of her character and genius to theirs. In the rest of this lecture let me remind you how exact that parallel is; how close—with certain essential differences—these resemblances are.

According to all the traditions of Israel the forefathers of the people came up from the Arabian desert into possession of the fertile lands of Syria; and in common with the early prose narratives the poetry reflects every phase in that change of physical environment through which such a passage necessarily brought them, every stage in the economic and social developments which it involved.

There is no exception to this, not even in the story of Abraham. Because the tradition describes him as starting upon his migration to Palestine from Ur of the Chaldees, one of the larger cities of Babylonia, it has been argued that the family or tribe to which he belonged were townsfolk already settled and (in the strict meaning of the word) civilised; and that Abraham fell back from this stage of culture upon the nomadic or at least the 'semi-nomadic'. Such a direction is difficult to conceive for any progressive breed of men [1]; nor do the premisses in Abraham's case compel us to conceive it of him. Ur of the Chaldees lay on the very edge of the settled country, near the mouth of one of the great avenues which lead up to this from the centre of Arabia. It is possible therefore, and, in the light of the patriarch's subsequent migrations, most reasonable, to assume that the stock from which he sprang was part of that second Semitic or Arabian invasion of Babylonia, to which archaeologists give the name of

[1] It must be allowed, however, that it is not impossible. The Beni Jafn of the first Christian century, who were said to have migrated from Yemen to the Roman frontier, had been nomads only during their desert wanderings, and brought with them to their new settlements memorials of their ancient culture. See V. Oppenheim's work cited in next note, i. p. 96.

'Canaanite', and that at the time when he broke from his people they had not yet firmly settled in Mesopotamia nor abandoned their nomadic habits. Distant migrations, such as Abraham is described achieving, have taken place between the Euphrates and the Nile within even recent times and devoid of the religious motives imputed to him.[1] But the tribes who have adventured upon them have been tribes which, though hovering in some cases upon the frontiers of civilisation, have not been settled in villages or towns. Nor do the traditions either of Abraham or his immediate descendants[2] show that they progressed in the inevitable transition to settlement further than many of the tribes whom to-day we call purely nomadic or semi-nomadic. Abraham, Isaac and Jacob are described roaming over great distances on, and even within, the borders of civilisation, and crossing the desert from Syria to Egypt and Egypt to Syria, just as some tribes, small and great, have been known to do within the last century. It is true that some of the patriarchs are represented as practising agriculture, but we are not told whether they did so by their own labours or by that of their slaves, or by forcing or hiring the peasants to work for them.[3] Abraham dwelt in tents and had to purchase a burial-place upon the settled soil. When his descendants came into Egypt they called themselves shepherds, that is nomads, desert-dwellers, a race alien to the settled Egyptians; and therefore Pharaoh assigned them a place for residence, not in the interior of Egypt, but upon the desert border, where they might continue their pastoral life. Again, Israel left Egypt utterly uninfluenced by the Egyptian civilisation. In the next lecture we shall see that some of their early poems, as well as some of the statements of the prophets,[4] represent them as still a desert people when found in the desert by their God and guided by Him to the fertile country promised to their fathers.

An even more significant piece of evidence is that the traditions impute to the incoming Israel two feelings which have always been characteristic of the nomads of the desert—the sense that the inhabitants of the fertile land were of a taller and heavier build than themselves, and a dread of walled cities.[5] Such statements cannot

[1] For such modern instances see Oppenheim, *Vom Mittelmeer zum Persischen Golf.*

[2] His nephew Lot is the one exception, drawn into 'the cities of the 'Arabah'.

[3] See above, p. 29.

[4] Hosea and Jeremiah.

[5] Num. xiii. 28–33; Deut. i. 28, ix. 1 f. Ancient Egyptian bas-reliefs represent the inhabitants of Palestine as bigger every way than the Arabs of the deserts. And at the present day any traveller who has spent some weeks among the latter will feel the same difference of height when he returns among the fellahin.

be the invention of Israelite historians writing centuries after Israel had dispossessed the Canaanite and the Amorite and had themselves settled to tillage. The feelings which these traditions impute could have been experienced only while Israel were still sons of the desert, a people of tents and without the nourishment of agriculture. Again—in spite of the tradition of the national unity under Moses before Palestine was reached—Israel are represented during the process of that invasion and after its achievement as still a number of loosely connected tribes. One of the strongest of these, Judah, was reinforced by, if indeed it did not entirely consist of, clans which for centuries resided on the desert border. Another tribe, Simeon, never left the desert. The whole nation was reminded that it inherited a civilisation which it did not create.[1] Customs and institutions, tempers and attitudes towards civilisation, religious conceptions and religious rites long persisted in Israel, some of which were identical with those of the desert nomads and some were strongly reminiscent of them. 'To your tents, O Israel' was still the national cry in the days of the kingdom. Long after the monarchy had created a central executive government among the people, with guards or police and prisons, the private vendetta, mitigated by a modified form of the right of asylum, was retained in the national law.

I have spoken of the 'Arab' character of Jacob, the father of the people. David and his troop of broken men lived the life of a desert tribe, inflicting blackmail on the peasantry. Amos, the first of the eighth-century prophets, was a desert shepherd with the nomad's hatred of buildings and scorn of luxury. And all through our period, although death is everywhere present and men are busy mourning and burying their dead, and although the records breathe a great and wistful tenderness on the subject, there reigns the same silence upon another life as we have marked among the Arabian nomads.

In the next lecture we shall see that all these things, thus hastily reviewed, are reflected in the early poetry of Israel: the desert circumstance and shepherd life; the desert tropes and figures; the desert theophanies; every phase of the inevitable transition to agriculture on a fertile soil with its effects on the nomad's appetite and imagination; the long survival of the nomadic habits and tempers; the purely tribal ethics and interests, the fertility of the tribe, its genealogies, its pride and its hatreds, its loyalties and sympathies, its relentlessness to enemies, its savage scorn and exultations; and, not least, all the nomad's strange silence—even in the

[1] Deut. vi. 10, 11.

moments of mourning when his heart is most vocal on the virtues of his dead—about another life for them.

We shall find, too, the same faculties and tempers of imagination: a terse, vivid realism combined with a 'subjective' or self-regarding treatment of all phenomena. We shall find—with a far less developed art of rhythm and metre—the same poetic styles, lyric, ballad, ode, proverb and riddle, with the same absence of epic; and a similar substitution for it of the prose story, compounded of many of the same elements found in that of the Arabs.[1]

But with all this likeness, even to detail, there are two strong differences: a sense of Israel's distinction, even of their uniqueness, among their fellow-nations, and, obviously as the cause of this, a spirit of religion, a progressive faith in God and His guidance of the people, for which we find no equivalent nor analogy in the poetry of the Arabs before Mohammed.

[1] Above, p. 38.

LECTURE III

SUBSTANCE AND SPIRIT (*continued*).

IN this lecture I have to show how far the early poetry of Israel reflects the circumstance, movements, and tempers of the life described in last lecture; and how it does so with many resemblances to Arabic poetry, but with these two differences: a sense of Israel's distinction from the other Semitic peoples of the period, and, what is obviously the cause of this, a growing confidence in God and in His guidance of the nation, to which there is no analogy in Arabic poetry before Mohammed.

I shall best accomplish my task by a translation of the poems as full, and as little interrupted by comment, as possible.

For preface I recall what was said about the dates of the poems.[1] A chronological arrangement of them is beyond our knowledge, and therefore I shall take them for the most part in the order in which they lie in the Old Testament. Till we get well down the series all dates are impossible. With the exception of the 'Blessing of Jacob',[2] parts at least of which reflect the conditions of the tribes of Israel after their settlement in Palestine, none of the poems quoted in the Book of Genesis afford any clear evidence of whether they were composed before that settlement or are later reflections upon traditions from the time to which they are assigned. All we can be sure of is that the verses are earlier than the prose documents which contain them—earlier, that is, than the ninth or eighth century. Their character is primitive, and except perhaps for the contrast between Israel's and Esau's lands, in Isaac's blessing of his sons, they contain nothing incompatible with a date before the settlement. Significant also is the character of the prose narrative, Genesis iv–xi, in which the first pieces are embedded. The religious spirit of this narrative is an ethical, and, except that it imputes to the Deity a jealousy of human powers and achievements, a lofty one. But this does not hide the original tempers of the traditions which are employed to point the morals. Cultivation is a punishment, and the fertile soil is under a curse; the discovery of wine is hailed as a relief. The progress of civilisation breeds arrogance, ending in disaster. The offering of

[1] See above, Introduction. [2] Ch. xlix.

Abel the shepherd is acceptable to God, that of Ḳain the cultivator is not, though the evidence here is curiously complicated by the fact that both are represented as standing on the fertile soil, and that it is the cultivator who is punished by being driven out upon the land of Nod, that is Nomad's-land, where blood revenge is the law—symptoms which betray the standpoint of the legend as in the cultivable country. More clearly the story of the Tower of Babel betrays that dislike of cities and horror of great buildings which we have seen to be characteristic of the tent-dwelling nomad. But the same hostility to civilisation appears in Israel as late as the eighth century, in the prophet Amos, himself a desert shepherd. So that it is impossible to say when the stories or poems which it inspires ceased to be composed in Israel. All we can affirm is that there is nothing in the poems—always excepting Jacob's and perhaps Isaac's blessing—which forbids a very ancient date. On the mixed character of the narratives, on the question whether they wholly reflect the settled conditions of Israel or contain some primitive elements, and on the questions of the relation of the poems to them, see the commentaries on Genesis and the monographs dealing with the subject.[1]

The very first verses, those attributed to Lamech, are also the rudest in spirit: one breathing the characteristic extravagance of the nomads in the pride of revenge, the other the first sense of introduction to the use of wine. The former, Gen. iv. 23, 24, has also, like so much Arab poetry, no thought of religion. The measure is irregular. The first couplet has four stresses to the line, or 4 : 3, according as you take the construct in the second line. The second couplet is 3 : 2, the third 3 : 3—

'Adhah and Ṣillah, hear ye my voice,
Give ear, Lémekh's-wives, to my speech,
A man have I slain for a wound to me,
And a boy for a blow to me.
For seven-fold avenged is Ḳain,
But Lamekh seventy and seven!

The Hebrew tense allows the alternative *I slay* in the third line; so that it is doubtful whether the singer celebrates a single act of vengeance or his general power and custom in that direction. In any case the song is the boast by a chief or a tribe[2] of that exaggeration to

[1] Of the latter especially Stade's in the *Zeitschrift zur A.T.lichen Wissenschaft*, 1894, 250 ff.; Wellhausen, *Die Composition des Hexateuch*; Budde's *Urgeschichte*; Gordon's *Early Narratives of Genesis*; of the former Gunkel's, Driver's, and Skinner's.

[2] If we retain the two women's names in the verse, which seems required by the metre, it is an individual who sings; if we leave them to the prose it may be a tribe addressing its w o m e n, which read for w i v e s.

which, as we have seen, the nomads carried the principle of the vendetta; it may be matched by similar Arab vaunts,[1] and like many of them, it is addressed to women. There are on record vows by Arab chiefs to slay 100 men in revenge for one, and a case in which this is said to have been done.[2] More relevant instances are found in the story of the famous war of el-Basûs which broke out on the murder of one Kulaib for the slaughter of a camel which had trespassed on the pasture of his clan. After much fighting between the tribes involved, Muhalhil, the brother of Kulaib, met Bujair, the son or nephew of a chief of the other side, el-Ḥārith, who had, however, refrained from taking part in the feud; and struck with his beauty, he asked him who he was. When he discovered this, he slew him, saying, 'Pay for Kulaib's shoe-latchet.' Ḥarith, desiring to stop the war, magnanimously refused to seek vengeance for Bujair's death. But Muhalhil repeated his boast, 'I have taken satisfaction only for Kulaib's shoe-latchet!' so Ḥarith broke out in verse—

> Bujair then was nought as a price for a slain man?
> . . . .
> A lord for a latchet, the price is too dear!—

and the feud flamed afresh.[3] Both this story and Lamech's song illustrate from what trifles the nomads' spirit of revenge might spread forth into prolonged and devastating wars.

Of late it has been usual to deny that the piece has any connection with the preceding prose record of the invention of metal weapons. The beginnings of the use of these by the nomads happened within historical times. The Egyptian monuments show to us Arabs armed only with wooden boomerangs, and a well-known Egyptian story describes the weapon-smiths journeying to them with their wares out of Egypt. In any case the narrator, by quoting Lamech's song at precisely this point, intended to emphasize the connection between the acquisition of the new art and the increased powers of revenge of which the song boasts. This is in harmony with the rest of his story. The rise in culture implies the better equipment of the immemorial right of the desert and its exaggerations by the nomads. But if that be so, what a weird reflection we find in those early days of the fatal services of modern science to international hatreds!

The other song attributed to Lamech, Gen. v. 29, also breathes

[1] Above, Lecture II, pp. 28, 30.

[2] For these instances see Jacob, *Altarabisches Beduinenleben*, 1897.

[3] The English reader will find the story in Lyall's *Ancient Arabian Poetry*, 6 f.; or at greater length in Nicholson's *Literary History of the Arabs*, 55 ff.

the spirit of the nomad, but on his introduction to a settled life of tillage and on his first experience of the benefits of the vine:

> This gives breath to us [1] from the toil of us
> And the pain of the hands of us.
> [From [2] the ground which Yahweh hath cursed].

The first two lines make a Ḳinah couplet, 3:2, with rhymes. Whether the last clause is also metrical and to be read as a third line is more than doubtful; it neither scans nor rhymes with the couplet. I take it as a prose gloss on the latter, explaining the toil and the pain.

The next pieces in our series,[3] Gen. ix. 25, and 26–27, are quoted in a story which gives a different impression of the effects of the vine: the story of Noah's drunkenness and the behaviour of his sons, Shem, Ham and Yapheth. The lines, whose origin is probably quite independent of the narrative, are curses on Canaan, identified by the narrator (who quotes them to point the moral of his narrative) with Ham, for his disgraceful treatment of his father. The first couplet is in 2:3—

> Cursed be K^{e}ná'an!
> Slaves'-slave shall he be to his brothers.

The text of the following is doubtful. As it stands and is confirmed by the Greek, it reads (in metre: 3 (or 4): 4:3:2:4)—

> Blessed be Yahwéh, Shem's-God,
> And K^{e}ná'an be slave to him! [4]
>
> God widen for Yápheth,
> That he dwell in Shem's tents,
> And K^{e}ná'an be slave to him! [4]

Professor Budde proposes, by omitting 'God' and a slight change of vowel, to read the first line:

> Blessed [5] of Yahweh [is] Shem,

while others conjecture

> Bless, Yahweh, Shem's tents.[6]

There is a play upon the name of Yapheth–yapht l^e Yepheth. The next line is ambiguous: to dwell in Shem's tents may be either a friendly or a hostile invasion.

[1] Heb. yenaḥ^{a}menu literally as above, and then = comforts, or relieves, us. Gk. read y^{e}nīḥenu = gives us rest: with a play on the word No^{a}ḥ.

[2] Or because of.

[3] The metrical fragments in the intervening chapters belong to the Priestly Document: e.g. Gen. ix. 6 (see p. 28).

[4] Or them.

[5] B^{e}ruk for baruk.

[6] So Graetz reading barek, and 'oh^{o}lē for '^{e}lohē.

But these questions of text and translation are as nothing compared to other questions started by the verses. What tribes or races are meant under the three names? What period of history is reflected by this description of their relations to each other? Shem must either be equivalent to Israel or inclusive of a group of peoples to which Israel belongs; for Yahweh is his God. Canaan or Kᵉnaʿan is likewise a group of tribes, some of whom were dispossessed by Israel and reduced to servitude. Yapheth is a name applied in the Old Testament to the northern and western nations *en masse*. But when did these oppress Canaan, or invade the tents of Shem either as friends or enemies? And why is such an invasion, especially if hostile, prayed for, or welcomed, by an Israelite singer?

To such questions one answer, very prevalent of late, is that the song reflects the condition of the people of Palestine during the most flourishing period of the Israelite monarchy, the same to which the prose narrative belongs. The highland Canaanites had then been finally reduced by Israel, and the coast Canaanites driven from their southern seats by the Philistines, with whom some accordingly identify Yapheth. Others take Yapheth to be the Phoenicians, who had peaceful relations with Israel soon after the settlement and again under Solomon and Ahab, and at the same time oppressed the Canaanites of the interior.[1] But this seems improbable in view both of the facts that the Phoenicians were themselves known to Israel at this time by the name of Canaan, and that there is no other sign of Israel being known by the name of Shem; and of the difficulty of conceiving how either the Philistines or the Phoenicians, under Yapheth or any other name, could be welcomed to Shem's tents by an Israelite singer. For this interpretation two substitutes have been offered. One[2] takes the verses as picturing certain racial relations in Syria during the second millennium B.C., for which there is some evidence. On this view Canaan stands for the first migration into Palestine from the east, which was pressed on to the coast by a second migration from the same quarter consisting of the Hebrew and Aramaic peoples here included under the name of Shem; while Yapheth stands for some northern race, perhaps the Hittites, pressing southwards upon both Canaan and Shem. This view is most attractive because of the evidence for the second millennium already referred to, and because it does justice to the character of the three names as names of races—and these primitive races—rather than of nations or tribes. But in

[1] For the Philistines, e.g. Wellhausen and Meyer; for the Phoenicians, Budde and more recently Holzinger.

[2] Gunkel, *Genesis*.

details this view is quite uncertain, and leaves unexplained Yapheth's welcome to the tents of Shem by a Shemitic bard. The other historical interpretation of the verses takes them as a whole, or at least as far as the reference to Yapheth is concerned, to be very late, reflecting the arrival in Palestine of the Greeks under Alexander, their subjugation of Phoenicia or Canaan, and their welcome by Jews.[1] But this interpretation also fails to account for some other features of the verses in the light of the actual conditions of the period. Where do the Persians come in? Why does a Jew of that time call his people Shem and not Israel? Or, to start the previous question, is it likely that a poem so late as the Greek period should have been inserted in one of the earliest documents of the Hexateuch?

To such difference of opinion is scholarship reduced by our ignorance of so much of the history of Israel!

But while these matters of fact must remain for the present uncertain, most clear and impressive are the interests and the spirit of the verses. Whatever their date may be, the poems reflect that interest of Israel in the characters and fortunes of foreign races, of which we shall find other instances in Hebrew poetry and to which there is no real analogy in the poetry of the Arabs. This interest, too, is religious, and towards Yapheth, sympathetic. On any reading of the text the verses welcome the introduction of some northern races to Israel's tents as by the hand of God Himself. There is the same readiness to rise at the sight of some historical movements—by us unfortunately unknown—to the conception of a universal Providence, which we see in the prophets of the eighth century and which is much more developed by them amid historical circumstances that we know in detail. Equally with the welcome to Yapheth, the curse on Canaan is the reflection of some historical situation. The context in which the narrator has set it shows that he, at least, felt the cause of Canaan's political inferiority to have been their low ethical temper. If we knew that the song was considerably earlier than the narrator's date—as evidently he implies—its religious attitude to Yapheth would stamp it as a document of the utmost importance in the history of the mind of Israel. Quite possibly it belongs to a date soon after the settlement, when Israel had begun, but had not achieved, the subjugation of the Canaanites; when the northern portion of these in Phoenicia were being simultaneously oppressed by peoples from further north; and the pious expectation was natural in Israel that such northern peoples would assist Israel in their overthrow of the hated race and dwell at peace with Israel in acknow-

[1] Bertholet, *Die Stellung der Israeliten u. der Juden zu den Fremden*, 198 f., &c.

ledgement of the same God, to whose Providence the events reflected were all felt to be due.

The other fragments in Genesis illustrate the characteristic interest of the Semites in tribal origins and genealogies and their desire for a numerous progeny.

The next in order is the oracle to Hagar, Gen. xvi. 11 f., before the birth of Ishmael.

And the angel of Yahweh said unto her,

Lo, thou art heavy, and bearing a son;
Call thou his name God-heareth,
For Yahwéh[1] hath heard thy distress.
Of mankind the wild-ass shall he be,
His hand against all, every hand against him,
From his brothers out East shall he dwell.

Literally 'out from the face of his brethren', but by Semitic orientation this means 'to the East' of them. For there the Arabs, the descendants of Ishma'el, dwelt; wild and hostile to their kinsfolk the settled Semites of Syria.

The next pieces are of Rebekah, Isaac, and their posterity; xxiv. 60: And they blessed Rebekah and said,

Our sister thou, become thousands, ten-thousands,
That thy seed may hold their foemen's gates.[2]

xxv. 23: And Yahweh said to her,

In thy womb are twin tribes,
Twin peoples shall break from thy body,
And a people than a people be stronger,
And the greater the smaller shall serve.

Then come Isaac's blessings on Jacob and Esau, xxvii. 27–29, 39–40: the first direct and the second ambiguous. The lines have, some two some three, stresses each. In the first 'fragrance' would be a better word than 'scent', but the latter has been chosen to bring out the alliteration of the original, r^{e}'eh re^{a}ḥ; one of the few alliterative lines which we shall meet with.

See, the scent of my son,
As the scent of a plentiful[3] field,
Which Yahweh[4] hath blessed.

[1] Possibly a later substitution for 'El = God.

[2] The phrase does not necessarily imply that Rebekah's people were settled in towns.

[3] So Greek and Vulgate. The rhythm, too, requires the additional accent.

[4] Again possibly for an original 'Ęl, God.

Give thee God from heaven's dew,
And from fats of the earth,
Wealth of corn and wine!
Serve thee the tribes,
Bow to thee peoples!
Be lord to thy brothers,
Thy mother's sons bow to thee!
Who curse thee be cursed,
And who bless thee be blessed!

And to Esau:

Lo, [far] from earth's fats
Thy dwelling shall be,
And [far] from the dew
Of heaven above.
On thy sword thou shalt live
But thy brethren serve.

A sentence has been added in prose from the later time when Edom threw off the sovereignty of Israel: 'And it shall be when thou hast the power thou shalt break his yoke from off thy neck'; clear proof that these poetical fragments are earlier than the narratives which quote them. But how much earlier?

The ambiguous 'from' is subtly used in these two pieces: positively in the first, but in the second in its privative sense; otherwise there would be no contrast between the fortunes of the two brothers. If this be the right interpretation, the land which is thought of for Esau cannot be that to the east of the 'Arabah of which he is said to have dispossessed the Ḥorim [1]; for this is not 'far from the dew and earth's fats', being in fact about as fertile as Israel's own. It must be that which was equally Esau's land to the west of the 'Arabah,[2] the wild desert south of the Negeb. Does this imply an early date for the piece?

The 'Blessing of Jacob' will be taken most suitably later on with its counterpart in Deut. xxxiii.

When we pass from the traditions of the Patriarchs to those of the origins of the nation from Egypt onwards to the settlement in Palestine, we are on firmer ground with regard to the events of the history and at the same time we find clearer reflections both of the changing environment of the migrant people and of their economic progress.

The first pieces are those in Exod. xv. 1 ff. and 20, 21, attributed to Moses and to Miriam. In the light of what we have learned of

[1] Deut. ii. 12.
[2] See the *Expositor*, Seventh Series, No. 34 (Oct. 1908), pp. 331 ff.

the authorship of Arab poems we shall not be prejudiced against the authenticity of such high names in the titles to these pieces. Much early Arabic poetry is genuine history, and the best of it was composed by doers, or spectators, of the deeds they chant.[1] But in Israel, as among the Arabs, it became the custom to add new verses to old poems, as well as to attribute to ancient names poems, whose dialect or contents prove them wholly to be late.[2] We must, therefore, examine the evidence which each poem offers apart from its title. In the Song of Moses this is of a mixed character. The latter part, verses 13–18, contains phrases which imply the settlement of the people in Palestine, and the establishment of their God in His sanctuary there. Moreover the prose note appended in verse 19 refers only to the earlier verses. In these, it is true, are several words and verbal forms not elsewhere found save in the Psalms and post-exilic writings[3]; but they are not therefore necessarily late, and nothing else disturbs the impression that the vivid verses are the celebration of the scene by one who has witnessed it.

Some notes are needed on the rhythm. Keeping in mind that the cardinal factor in Hebrew verse is its Parallelism,[4] we divide the lines accordingly and find that most of them are of two stresses each. This is true even of verse 6, for though at first it seems to have two lines of four stresses each, these are divisible by a caesura and between the halves also there is a pause in the sense. Similarly in the opening sentence of verse 7. By such a division, too, we secure a regularity of couplets throughout; without it the first line of verse 7 becomes a third to the two of verse 6, whereas it belongs properly to the couplet which follows it, as the pronominal suffix at the end of this couplet distinctly shows. Similarly the third and fourth lines of verse 1, unless they are separated, become a third line to the opening couplet. We may, therefore, safely take two stresses to the line as the normal measure of the poem. But there are also a few lines of three stresses: in verse 2 the first, in 5 the second, and in 8 the third and fourth—all these indubitably; with perhaps also the first of verse 4.[5]

We shall find the same metre—normally of two stresses to the line

[1] Above, Lecture II, pp. 36, 37.

[2] Some psalms which in the Hebrew canon are anonymous bear in the Greek version the names of famous men. For the Arab analogies see above, p. 36.

[3] Deeps (t^ehomōth), depths (m^eṣōlōth), streams (noz^elīm), heart of the sea, flash my sword, and the terminations -enhū, -āmō and -ēmō.

[4] Above, Lecture I, pp. 13, 17.

[5] For the heavy construct, chariots-of-Pharaoh, needs almost certainly two stresses.

but varied by lines of three stresses—in parts of the Song of Deborah; and the variety is to be explained on the grounds given in Lecture I.[1]

One line is alliterative, the third of verse 8, and one couplet is rhymed, the last of verse 9. As far as possible I reproduce these features in the following translation. But sometimes a Hebrew line of two accents can only be given in English with three, as in the second line of this poem.

1. Then sang Moses and the sons of Israel this Song of Yahweh and they said,

Yahwéh I sing,
High hath He triumphed.
The horse and his rider
He hurled in the sea.

2. Strength of me, song of me Yah,
He is my succour.
My God, I praise Him,
My sire's-God, exalt Him.

3. Yahwéh, man of war,
Yahwéh His name.

4. Phar'oh his chariots, his host,
He poured in the sea,
The choice of his captains
Were plunged in the Red-sea.

5. The deeps overwhelmed them,
To the depths they went down like a stone.

6. Thy right hand, Yahwéh,
O glorious in might;
Thy right hand, Yahwéh,
It shatters the foe.

7. In the wealth of Thy triumph,
Thou tear'st Thine opponents.
Thou launchest Thy wrath,
It eats them like stubble.

4. Plunged, or better dumped, ṭubbeʿū; the use of the root in Arabic, &c., proves that the original sense of this onomatopoeic word was to stamp or dump down, like the die upon the coin. Captains: Driver, knights: the rank is uncertain.

6. Glorious, lit. showing Himself glorious. The masc. form proves that unlike the next verb it refers to Yahweh not to His hand.

[1] pp. 17, 18.

8. By the blast of Thy nostrils
Heaped were the waters,
Stayed like a stack as they streamed,
Stark were the deeps to the heart of the sea.

9. The foe had said,
'I chase, I make,
I cast the spoil,
My lust they glut,
I flash my brand,
Ousts them my hand!'

10. Thou blewest with Thy wind,
Ocean o'erwhelmed them;
Sank they like lead
In the glorious waters.

The song of Miriam (xv. 20 f.) is a tiny fragment, but with the prose introduction to it tells us almost as much as the song of Deborah about the conceptions of poetry which prevailed in early Israel.

And Miriam the prophetess, the sister of Aaron, took a toph (or timbrel) in her hand, and all the women went after her with timbrels and with dances, and Miriam chanted—that is, chanted in antiphon—to them:

Sing to Yahwéh,
High hath He triumphed;
The horse and his rider
He hurled in the sea.

8. I am not sure of the line-division of this verse given above. The sentence I have made two lines can only be so divided by giving two stresses to the construct phrase. Give them but one and the sentence is one line with three accents, like the two lines which follow it; and the verse becomes a triplet. The third line has a three-fold alliteration. Stayed, stopped or stood still; Stark were, or curdled, congealed, condensed, became solid.

9. After the three-stress lines of verse 8 the resumption of a two-stress measure for the vaunts of the foe is effective, especially as the unaccented syllables at first are few. We get the impression of an eager, almost panting voice. The last two lines rhyme but only on the pronominal suffix for my, and therefore not so distinctly as in the above translation. I flash ('arīk) usually rendered I draw, as though 'empty' the scabbard of the sword. But both here and in the passages in Ezekiel, in which the phrase occurs, the context implies a more thorough action than the mere drawing of the sword. The Arabic analogue suggests either 'I make my sword to flash', or 'I pour it out, sweep right and left with it'. (Cf. our phrase, 'to rain blows.')

10. They sank. The word ṣal^{a}lū is onomatopoeic (in Arabic it is used of gurgling water), and hissed or whistled would come nearer to the sound it conveys. But lead does not whistle on falling into water. Gurgled is better; yet sank itself somewhat echoes the sound intended. Driver, whizzed down.

Some years ago I travelled for a few days in the deserts of Judaea under the protection of a Bedawee tribe. The guides they gave us were the chief's son and brother, with five other men. At Engedi we reached the limits of their territory, where we had to take fresh guides from another tribe. So they made for us what the Arabs call a 'fantasia'. It was bright moonlight. The seven of them stood up with the same instrument as the toph of Miriam and her women, and of the same name, daff[1]; and began a slow dance to the accompaniment of their music. In a little the chief's son—mark you, no professional minstrel but the principal personage among them—stood out from the rest and, still dancing, chanted an improvised verse descriptive of our journey. His fellows caught it and sang it back to him. He followed with other verses, thirty or thirty-five in all, each describing some phase of the journey, or some aspect of the landscapes through which we had passed, with allusions to the virtues of his tribe, and, of course, with hints at our own still prospective liberality. The chorus did not always repeat the first verse; but when a fresh one of superior quality was improvised by the young chief they caught at that, and for the next few verses made it the refrain. And all the time they danced and one of them played their timbrel.

Here was the very kind of poetry which we find in the account of Miriam's song, and in fact among all primitive peoples. To them poetry is not merely the arrangement in regular measures of vivid, musical words; nor is the composition of it left to the professional poet. Song is not the work of the voice alone. Early peoples expected in poetry what we seek from our orators, that the whole body shall contribute to the rhythm; that music shall always accompany it; that it shall be the product of experience rather than of imagination; that no strange heart or voice is sufficient for it, but that the very head, hands and limbs which have done the actions celebrated shall spring, warm and rhythmical, from the doing of the things to the singing of them. Of such poetry we may say that it is just the peroration of life; and that after all must be the vividest poetry.

The narratives of the wilderness enclose a singularly small number of verses; and first a fragment on the war with 'Amalek, Exodus xvii. 15, 16: And Moses built an altar and called its name Yahweh-Nissi (my standard), and he said:

[1] The daff (or ṭār) is the tambourine or timbrel, skin tightly bound over a hoop, in which loose metal plates are inserted. A similar instrument is the hand-drum darabukkeh, a jar of pottery with a skin bottom. It is to me uncertain which of these was the Hebrew toph.

On Yah's standard a hand,
Yahwéh at war,
With 'Amalék for ever![1]

The next two are the lines on the lifting and resting of the Ark, Numbers x. 35, 36: And it was when the Ark was lifted that Moses said:

Arise, Yahwéh,
That Thy foes be scattered
And Thy haters flee from Thy face.[2]

And when it rested he would say:

Return, Yahwéh,
To the myriads,[3] the clans of Isra'el.

There is also the oracle to Aaron and Miriam when they had spoken against Moses, Numbers xii. 6–8. The lines are irregular, of two or three stresses each. And Yahweh said to them[4]:

Hear now My words!
Be a prophet among you,
By visions I make Me be known to him,
And by dreams with him do I speak.
Not so is My servant, Moshéh,
Of My house most trusted is he.
Mouth to mouth with him do I speak,
Not in vision[5] nor by riddles.
[And the form of Yahwéh he beholds]
Why then feared ye not—
To speak 'gainst My servant, Moshéh?

It is always a question whether a poem is older than the narrative in which it occurs, or the narrative than the poem with the poem composed to fit it. In this case the oracle seems (from its second line) to have been addressed to a larger audience than Miriam and Aaron, the culprits in the accompanying story, and may have originally belonged to the tradition of a wider revolt against the authority of Moses. The language betrays nothing late, nor do the ideas; unless it be held that the more rational form of prophecy, as distinguished from that which worked by ecstasy or dreams, did not

[1] Hand, sign or indicator. Standard: for kes read nes, which seems necessary after verse 15. For ever, Heb. from age to age.

[2] The last is a swell-line.

[3] Others read, and bless.

[4] So one Greek version and the Syriac. Yahweh in the second line of the Hebrew text is contrary both to sense and metre, and may have slipped there from here.

[5] Hebrew has without a negative the word mar'eh, vision, as in the third line, but here to be taken adverbially as if clearly or plainly. If this be the correct reading, then we have an instance of the use in these early oracles of an ambiguous word in both its meanings.

appear in Israel before the age of Samuel. Against so dogmatic a conclusion, and in support of the possibility of a contemporary date for the poem, we may set the strong witness of the traditions to the personality of Moses and to the character of his work for Israel; as well as the fact that among the Semites poems were frequently the only records of events, and that they did deliver the truth about these as well as contemporary impressions of men and nature. But certainty on the point is impossible. The curious line, *and the form of Yahwéh he beholds*, is doubtful. It is the only *third* line in the piece, all the rest are in couplets, and it seems an afterthought.

These are all the verses which the earliest narratives refer to the wilderness. But the narratives are themselves full of the desert's poetry. Their theophanies and miracles are the theophanies and the miracles of the desert. The first appearance of the Deity to Moses is on the Semitic wilderness and in one of its common bushes.[1] That the glory of the Lord should have first shone to him and that the Lord should have first spoken to him, not from some palm or whispering oak of the fertile soil, but from an ordinary desert bush, the characteristic vegetation of the Arabian wilderness; and that this, while it burned with the glory of God, was nevertheless not consumed, is a fit symbol of the religion of Israel from first to last. For that religion glowed with an authentic Divine fire, not seen elsewhere in the Semitic world; yet its roots were in the desert soil, and in stock and fibre, in rites and institutions it remained essentially Semitic still. A later poet, blessing the tribe of Joseph after they had settled on a fruitful territory, wishes for them in climax to other blessings,

The favour of the Bush-dweller.[2]

The other theophany of these early days is the thunderstorm, a favourite theophany of Arabian poets[3]: the mountain enveloped with cloud and burning with fire; and some of the earliest poems salute the appearance of God from the same region and in the same figures, adding that of the rain. So in the opening of the Song of Deborah[4]:

Yahwéh, at Thine outset from Se'ír,
On Thy march from the range of 'Edhóm,
Earth did quake,
Heaven swayed,
Clouds poured water,
Hills shook down at Yahwéh,
Yahwéh, Isra'el's-God.

[1] Exod. iii. 1 ff.

[2] Deut. xxxiii. 16.

[3] See above, Lecture II, p. 3.

[4] Judges v. 4-5.

Or the opening of the song in Deuteronomy xxxiii:

Yahweh from Sinái did come,
And rose from Se'ír upon them.
He shone from the Mount of Parán,
And broke from Merībath-Ḳadésh

. . . .

From the south fire . . . them.[1]

These facts, that the thunderstorm was a favourite theophany of the nomad Semites; that it occurs in what are admitted to be very early Hebrew poems; that all the memories of the people trace the dominant revelation of their God to the thunders of Sinai; and that (towards the end of our period) Elijah is bidden to look for the presence of God no longer in the thunder and other violent forces of nature but in some spiritual manifestation—these facts suggest the following question. Do the Psalms and other poems in the Old Testament which chant of similar theophanies likewise belong to our period; before Israel had cast off the influences of the mythology characteristic of the desert, and by long settlement in sight of a maritime coast, and by their contact with Babylonian culture had come under the influence of those mythologies of the sea and the delta, which prevail in the later poetry of the Old Testament? To so interesting a question there is no certain answer. But it is worth noting that except at the crossing of the Red Sea [2] there is no reference in our poetry to the mythical powers of the Ocean; and that two of the Psalms which celebrate the appearance of Yahweh in thunderstorms, the Eighteenth and Twenty-ninth, are both ascribed to David; the former, be it remembered, even by some scholars who deny the certainty of any other Davidic Psalm.

The relevant verses of Psalm xviii are very powerful. Earthquake and thunderstorm are mingled, but notice how the former is felt only at the beginning and end of the piece. Between these the thunderstorm dominates—dominates even the earthquake, which is stilled till it has passed. Never was a more sublime theophany. The equal massiveness and rapidity of the clouds, the awful darkness, the thought of the pent-up waters packing the heavens, the flash of the God's approach, the thundering, the zigzags crossing and shivering through each other, the ravel of the lightnings—all is described in a way which defies translation. And the effect might be more stupendous if the text were firmer and we understood

[1] The last two lines emended partly after the Greek.

[2] And there only to Tehom or Tehomoth, which forms, some argue, imply a late date for 'The Song of Moses', Exod. xv. 1-10. See above, p. 51 *n.* 3.

better some of the separate phrases. It is noteworthy that the meaning of one at least of these[1] was already forgotten by later scribes, and can be restored only from the Arabic, a symptom not unfavourable to the theory of an early date.

The lines are normally of three stresses each, but as usual there are a few variations. The verses are couplets, except three which are triplets. There is no rhyme except in the two verbs of the first line, nor alliteration except in the first two words of verse 12. Another edition of the text is found in 2 Samuel xxii.

7. Earth was shaking and quaking,
The bases of heaven did tremble,
They reeled, for that He was wroth.
8. A smoke went up from His nostrils,
And fire from His mouth devoured,
Out of Him brimstones were kindled.
9. And He bowed the heavens and came down,
And the storm-cloud was under His feet.
10. And He rode on a Cherub and flew,
And swept on the wings of the wind.
11. Darkness He set for His ambush,
Round about Him His covert,
With the pent-up waters packed were the clouds.
12. At the brightness before Him they kindled,
Burst through the lightning (?) and brimstones.

7. The first two verbs rhyme, wattig'ash wattir'ash. Heaven, so in 2 Sam. xxii, our text reads mountains. In line three the verb is a heavier form of the first verb in line one; see above, p. 20.

8. Brimstones, i. e. in the original sense of burning stones.

10. Cherub, Heb. Kᵉrūbh, the mythical wind monster.

11. In the second and third lines the text is uncertain and the metre broken. It is not clear how the lines are to be divided. The phrase of the text darkness of waters, ḥeshkath-maim is improbable. I propose ḥeskath-maim from ḥasak, to hold up, restrain: for the same verb in Arabic, ḥashak, is used of clouds full of water, and of excessive rain. Trans. gathering of waters or as above pent-up waters. So in 2 Sam. xxii, but with another radical ḥashrath (?). Also the Greek of 2 Sam. reads a verb in the third line. Instead of 'abhē, clouds or masses of, I propose therefore 'abhū, were thick or packed. In any case the line is a heavier one than the preceding two with which it forms a triplet. The metre is irregular and the lines might alternatively be divided thus:

His covert around Him the pent-up waters,
Packed were the clouds.

12. Text and meaning again uncertain. As it stands the Hebrew confirmed by the Greek gives two irregular lines: At the brightness before Him His clouds passed away (or through)—Hail and brimstones of fire. In 2 Samuel, Hebrew and Greek have the defective—At the brightness before Him they kindled—. ... brimstones of fire. By reading the first line as in 2 Samuel, and transferring the verb of our Psalm to the second line, we get as above a regular metre and a natural meaning. But Hebrew and Greek both read barad, hail; at this point we expect rather baraḳ, lightning, which therefore is suggested above.

[1] See the note on verse 11.

13. Yahwéh did thunder from heaven,
The Highest uttered His voice.
14. He shot out His arrows and strewed them,
He hurled the lightnings and ravelled them.
15. The beds of the waters were seen,
And bared were the world's foundations—
At Thy rebuke, Yahwéh,
The blast of the breath of Thy nostrils.

The other description of the appearance of God in a thunderstorm, the Twenty-ninth Psalm, describes the progress of the storm from the peaks of Lebanon down the mountain-flanks and out upon the desert. I quote with it, for comparison and contrast, a celebrated Arabic poem on the same subject. The two describe similar directions and similar effects of the storm. But the Arab contents himself with these and, unlike the Hebrew, sees no theophany. The art of his presentation is superior to the Hebrew's, and he is a far greater master in metre, like all his kind, as might be expected from their much later date. I give the Arab poem, which is by the famous Imra el-Ḳais (died *circa* 540 A.D.), in Sir Charles Lyall's admirable translation:

O Friend—see the lightning there! it flickered and now is gone,
as though flashed a pair of hands in the pillar of crownèd cloud.
Nay, was it its blaze, or the lamps of a hermit that dwells alone
and pours o'er the twisted wicks the oil from his slender cruse?

We sat there, my fellows and I, 'twixt Ḍarij and al-'Udhaib,
and gazed as the distance gloomed, and waited its oncoming.
The right of its mighty rain advanced over Ḳaṭan's ridge,
the left of its trailing skirt swept Yadhbul and as-Sitâr;

Then over Kutaifah's steep the flood of its onset drave,
and headlong before its storm the tall trees were borne to ground;
And the drift of its waters passed o'er the crags of al-Ḳanân,
and drave forth the white-legged deer from the refuge they sought therein.

And Taimá—it left not there the stem of a palm aloft,
nor ever a tower, save one firm built on the living rock.
And when first its misty shroud bore down upon Mount Thabîr,
he stood like an ancient man in a grey-streaked mantle wrapt.

13. The text gives a third line, a careless repetition of *hail and brimstones of fire* from the previous verse.

14. *Them* and *them* at the ends of the two lines can only refer here to the arrows and the lightnings, and not, as is usually implied, to the enemies of the Psalmist, for these have not been mentioned since verse 3. Therefore the usual translation of the verbs by *scattered* and *discomfited* is wrong. The second line describes vividly, and accurately, the mixed and hustled flashes of a lavish lightning, the zigzags leaping into and across each other. The Greek favours this view by its *multiplied* for *hurled*: *lavished and ravelled the lightnings*.

15. *Waters*: in 2 Samuel, *the Sea*.

The clouds cast their burden down on the broad plain of al-Ghabîṭ,
as a trader from al-Yaman unfolds from the bales his store;
And the topmost crest on the morrow of al-Mujaimir's cairn
was heaped with the flood-borne wrack like wool on a distaff wound.

At earliest dawn on the morrow, the birds were chirping blithe,
as though they had drunken draughts of riot in fiery wine;
And at even the drowned beasts lay where the torrent had borne them, dead,
high up on the valley sides, like earth-stained roots of squills.

The Hebrew Psalm, of uncertain date, opens like the narrative poems of our period, with praise to God, and to its praise it returns after the description of the storm, for it hears God through the whole course of the latter.[1] Mark how both the Arab and the Hebrew close their descriptions with the havoc wrought on the beasts, and give, in contrast to this, the Arab the singing birds on earth, the Hebrew the singing angels in heaven:

1. Give to Yahwéh, ye sons of God,
Give to Yahwéh the glory and might.
2. Give to Yahwéh of His name the glory,
Worship Yahwéh in holy estate.

3. Yahwéh His voice is out on the waters,
The God of glory doth thunder!
Yahwéh out on the waters great.
4. Yahwéh His voice in power, Yahwéh His voice in splendour.

5. Yahwéh His voice breaking the cedars,
Yahwéh shattereth Lebanón's cedars.
6. Maketh them spring—like a calf Lebanón,
And Siryón like to a wild-ox.

7. Yahwéh His voice hewing out flames,
[Yahwéh] . . . .
8. Yahwéh His voice makes the wilderness whirl,
Yahwéh makes whirl the wilds of Ḳadésh.

9. Yahwéh His voice starts the hinds to their pangs,
[Yahwéh] He layeth naked the woods.
. . . .
While in His palace all uttereth glory.

10. Yahwéh on the flood is enthroned,
Yahwéh enthroned, King for ever.
11. Yahwéh will give strength to His folk,
Yahwéh will bless His people with peace.

[1] Cheyne and Baethgen recall the echo of this Psalm in the hymns of the three archangels in Goethe's *Faust*, especially Michael's.

'Hewing out flames' may mean 'hewing them out of the clouds'; but it is possible to translate 'splitting' or 'cleaving' the flames, and then it refers to the zigzags of the lightning. 'Makes the wilderness whirl' seems to describe the dust rising in lofty spirals, as it does in the van of a storm; but others refer the phrase to the inhabitants of the wilderness. 'Layeth naked the woods' is usually interpreted of the stripping of the leaves, but it seems to me rather to describe—and very vividly—the effect of the lightning, the recesses of the forest flashing naked beneath it. So would the hinds be startled into premature birth-pangs.

The metre is worth close examination; it is an instructive example of the difficulties that attend the analysis of Hebrew rhythm. Usually this metre is defined as one of four stresses to the line; but this is true, true indubitably and past question, of only five of the lines as they stand: the second, the fifth last, and the last three. Others meet the requirement only if we give the construct (or genitive) phrases *two* stresses instead of *one*, as for example, in the first, third, and tenth lines; while others only if we give the same, or similar, constructs one accent, as in the eighth and thirteenth lines; while again other lines cannot upon any arrangement have more than three stresses each, like the sixth line or the fourth from the end. There is no doubt about the text of these lines. The only solution of the difficulty is to accept the irregularities as originally designed to give variety to the metre, or to suppose that, as with the modern songs of Palestine, the shorter lines had stresses added to them in the singing or recitation of the piece.[1]

The lines divide into six quatrains, but of these only the first three and the last are complete. The second line of the fourth is missing; the first line should have a parallel with the simple 'Yahweh' as its nominative. Dr. Cheyne proposes:

> The voice of Jehovah hews [the rocks]
> [hews them with] flames of fire,

and similarly Dr. Duhm. So, too, there are but three lines to the fifth verse, and a parallel is wanting to the last of them. But it is possible, that for the sake of variety both verses were purposely left as triplets.

The thunderstorm has swept us far from our course of following the series of poems ascribed to Israel's migration between Egypt to the Promised Land, and to this series I now return as it crosses the border of Moab. To the wanderings on the actual desert the

[1] See above, Lecture I, p. 18.

narratives assign, as we have seen, but few fragments of verse. But when Israel reach the borders of cultivation the songs become as more numerous in the narrative as the springs do on the line of the people's march; and there is a large and lively group connected with their experiences in Moab. The first, Num. xxi. 14, 15, cited from the Book of the Wars of Yahweh, is a provoking piece, for it is the only fragment which Hebrew tradition has preserved of the music of the march, a music conspicuous and charming in the poetry of the nomad Arabs. The narrator does not ascribe his quotation to Moses or any contemporary minstrel, but merely notes: 'Therefore it is said in the Book of the Wars of Yahweh.'[1] This may be taken for evidence that the song appeared in the Book without any statement of its origin, or as betraying that the lines quoted from it were torn out of associations of a different kind from those of the present narrative; and such a reading is supported by the ragged abruptness of the lines themselves. The questions thus raised are interesting, but cannot be answered on the meagre evidence before us. One of the most interesting of them, that of the narrator's method of quotation, may be better discussed when we come to the next song but one. In any case, as we shall see, the lines reflect the actual scenery of Israel's march through southern Moab.[2] The measure is uncertain, but appears to be of two and then of three stresses to the line; but Prof. Holzinger takes verse 15 as a line of seven stresses, and infers that what precedes it is a broken line of the same measure:

14*b*. Wahéb in Supháh
And the valleys, 'Arnón,
15. And the cliff of the valleys,
Which stretches to 'Ar's-seat
And leans on the verge of Mo'áb.

Waheb and the valleys are in the accusative case and require a verb to govern them. The Greek translators, besides reading Zahab for Waheb, found instead of in Suphah a verb, he burned.[3] The

[1] See above, Introduction.

[2] Holzinger's contention (in his commentary and in Kautzsch's translation) that, as the lines are quoted from the Book of *Wars*, the poem of which they are a fragment must have celebrated a war of Israel on Moab and therefore cannot have described Israel's peaceful march under Moses by the borders of Moab, but was probably a later production celebrating an invasion of Moab from the north by an Israelite king—is unfounded. For the poem, while mainly about Israel's previous or subsequent wars, may have included a brief description of the people's easy passage across the obstacles presented by the valleys of Arnon. These (note the plural) are in *southern* Moab, and that was a region which appears never to have been conquered by Israel in the times of the monarchy. The Israelite border is always at Aroer on the north bank of Arnon.

[3] Τὴν Ζωὸβ ἐφλόγισεν = eth-Zahab saraph.

verb, however, may have been another; the Hebrew suggests Saphah, he swept—up or away, which root in Arabic means also was swift in going. It is possible, therefore, that the first couplet originally ran:

> Wahéb he hath swept (or scoured)
> And the valleys, 'Arnón.

Waheb or Zahab is quite unknown; we expect rather Zered, the wady crossed by Israel before the Arnon.[1] Valleys not valley, for the name 'Arnon—probably derived, like its modern substitute Mojib, from the noise of falling streams,—covered a complex of wadies uniting in the long, deep trench that carries their waters to the Dead Sea. Their cliffs are conspicuous, especially those of the main branch, whose north wall was the frontier of Moab—

> Leans on the verge of Mo'áb—

and stretches east to the site of the formidable ruins now known as Mdeyyneh, which Herr Musil has reasonably identified with the 'Ir, or city of, Mo'ab, and this was certainly the same as the 'Ar-Mo'ab, or 'Ar of our fragment, standing on the extremity of the border.[2]

We find then in the verse the same qualities as distinguish the Arab songs of travel: a list of place-names but each set musically and along with some vivid detail of the scenery in which it lies. If, however, the subject of the verb be not a man or men, as in the Arab songs, and this piece, like so many others in the early poetry of Israel, describes the march of God Himself; then perhaps those are right who take the last clause not as a line of the poem but as a topographical gloss attached to it.[3]

The next piece is the Song of the Well, Num. xxi. 17, 18. Like the last it is the only specimen of its kind preserved in the Old Testament; though, again, that kind must have been as common in Israel as we have found it among the Arabs.[4] The metre has two stresses to each of the first two lines and three to each of the rest.

And from thence [Israel came] to B^{e}'er, the B^{e}'er of which Yahweh said to Moses, 'Gather the people and I will give them water.' Then sang Israel this song:

> Spring up, O Well!
> Sing ye back to her.
> Well princes dug her,
> Delved her the lords of the folk
> With sceptres, with their staves.

[1] Identified by Musil, *Moab*, p. 361, with the upper stretch of the Wady es-Sulṭani, one of the feeders of the Arnón.

[2] See article by the present writer in the *Expositor* for August, 1908, pp. 138, 139.

[3] So Holzinger, *in loco*.

[4] Above, p. 32.

Some have thought to read in these lines the custom of divining for water by the rod, but the terms delved and dug are too honest for that fancy; and Herr Musil has confirmed the obvious sense of the words by his recent report of the habits of certain Arabs on the borders of Moab. He says that in the Wady eth-Thamad, the upper stretch of the Wady Waleh, itself a northern tributary of the 'Arnon, the Arabs dig out with their hands pits in the gravel of the dry torrent bed, in which water gathers. 'Such water-pits are called Bīr, Biyâr. Since they are regularly filled up [with gravel] by the winter rains, they have to be freshly dug every spring. Each tent possesses its own bīr; those of the heads of families and clans are restored with special care, and although the chiefs only seldom work themselves and with their own hands, yet it is always said: This well dug (ḥafar[1]) Sheikh N.'[2]

So much for the custom. It is at least a curious coincidence that Herr Musil should have seen it practised in the very neighbourhood to which the Hebrew story assigns this song. 'It is', he says, 'the only place north of the Arnon where the water comes to the surface in the manner described in Numbers xxi. 16–18. Eth-Thamad gives exactly the meaning of the Hebrew Beʼer,[3] and the terebinths growing here justify the epithet Elim.' He therefore identifies the spot, 'el-Mdeyyne on eth-Thamad', with the Israelite station Beʼer and with the Beʼer ʼElim of Isaiah xv. 8. The distance, too, from the 'Arnon, presumably Israel's previous camp, is quite suitable. But it is difficult to believe that such methods of procuring water are not applicable in other wadies on the desert border, as they certainly are elsewhere; and terebinths are frequently found in Moab.

The two words following the song in the text, usually understood as part of the prose itinerary, Professor Budde takes as an additional line to the song—

From the desert a gift!

This is a suitable close, and in fact gives the needed parallel to the fifth line. Like each of the first two lines it has two stresses.[4]

The next piece is given in connection with Israel's war against Sihon, the king of the Amorites, Num. xxi. 27–30.[5] Unlike its

[1] The same verb as the first of the two given in the song.

[2] *Moab*, p. 298.

[3] Cf. Lane, *sub voce* Thamad, 'water retained beneath the sand and when this is removed is yielded by the ground,' and in the plural, 'holes dug or excavated in which there is a little water.' But note that W. el-Ḥsa has a similar meaning.

[4] If the line be adopted the letter *waw* with which it opens must be transferred to the end of the fifth line, elongating the suffix there.

[5] On the question of the historical value of the prose narrative of this war see

fellows in these narratives, it is quoted neither from older Books nor with the name Moses or any author, but simply as wont to be sung by bards: 'Therefore the Moshelim—those that sing mashâls—are wont to say.' The absence of an author's name—as also in the introduction to the fragment on the Valleys of the Arnon—is evidence that the narrator or editor did not improve, at least *not always*, upon tradition when quoting an older song, but left it, at least sometimes, as anonymous as he found it. So far as it goes, such evidence is in his favour and supports the belief that when he did put a name to a poem he had some tradition for this. Nor does he even say, as in some other cases, that the piece was composed or sung at the time of the events to which he attaches it. He may have thought so, as seems indicated by his 'therefore'. But this somewhat naïve expression, frequently used in these historical narratives to attach to an event the dubious meaning of a place-name, or the origin of a proverb, raises the suspicion that he had before him no tradition which connected our song with the war against Sihon; and this becomes more significant when we find that the only unambiguous verse in the song (30) describes not Sihon and the Amorites but Moab, the people of Kemosh, as the victims of the conquest celebrated; and further, that the course of this conquest is traced not from south to north, the direction of Israel's advance, but from north to south (28 and apparently also in 29). Some have therefore taken the song to be not of Hebrew but of Amorite origin, celebrating not the victory of Moses over Sihon but the previous victory of Sihon over Moab. Others support the reference to Israel's war with Sihon by taking the first couplet (27) as addressed by Israel either to themselves or, in derision, to the Amorites; the next verses (28, 29) as descriptive of Sihon's previous conquest of Moab from the north [1]; and the last (30) as Israel's renewed exultation in their rout of Sihon. This is somewhat artificial; and in particular, while the text of verse 30 is very uncertain, the only reliable words in it, Heshbon to Dibon, point like the rest to an advance from north to south. Others, again, read the poem as celebrating an invasion of Moab from the north by Omri or another Israelite monarch. In this case, however, the words 'to the king of the Amorites' must be taken as a later intrusion; and indeed they form an odd, unmatched line among the otherwise parallel couplets. The theory also implies that the Sihon of the opening

Gray and Holzinger in their commentaries; Kittel's *History*, ii. 228–31; and the present writer's *Hist. Geog. of the Holy Land*, Appendix III.

[1] In the first line of 28 the position of the verb makes it possible to take it as a pluperfect; but this, which would be necessary in the syntax of prose, is not necessary in verse.

couplets was not the Amorite but a king of Moab: of such a monarch there is no trace elsewhere. One great difficulty is the ambiguity of the second couplet: it may either mean that the invasion started from Heshbon and was therefore Sihon's, or first attacked Heshbon and may therefore have been inflicted by a king of Israel.

The metre is partly of two, partly of three stresses to the line.

27b. Come, let Heshbón be rebuilt,
And restored the town of Sihón!

28. For fire went forth from Heshbón,
Flame from the burgh of Sihón.
It devoured ʿAr—Mo'áb,
It swallowed the heights of 'Arnón.

29. Woe t' thee, Mo'áb,
Perished thou, folk of Kᵉmósh!
He hath given his sons to flight,
And his daughters to exile.
[To the Amorite king, Sihón.]

30. Their offspring (?) is perished,
From Heshbón to Dibón.
The[ir] women are . . . .
[From?] . . . . to the desert.

In verse 30 (see the foot-note) the text has become very corrupt and a certain restoration of it is impossible. The fragments given are from the versions. It might—but this is pure conjecture—be completed thus:

Their offspring is perished
From Heshbón to Dibón,
Their women are childless
From the Slopes[1] to the Desert.

This gives the extent of northern Moab in both directions: from north

28. Swallowed, so Gk. reading balʿah for the Heb. baʿalē, the lords of.

29. He, i. e. their God Kemosh. The phrases are the same as are used of Yahweh and Israel.

The fifth line, as remarked above, is the one odd line among parallel couplets, and probably a later intrusion.

30. Their offspring, so Gk. reading nīnam; Vulg. nīram, their lamp (cf. 1 Kings xi. 36); Heb. nīram, we shot them, but both the parallelism and the immediately following verb require a noun. From, so Vulg. [Their] women. so Gk. nashim or nᵉshēhem, Heb. nashshim, we laid [them] waste. The Heb. continues unintelligibly to Nophah which [is] to Medeba; and the Gk. equally so: still kindled fire upon Moab. For the Heb. Medᵉba the Pesh. reads Midbar, desert, which has been adopted above.—For other emendations, based on his theories of Miṣṣur, see Cheyne, *Critica Biblica* and *Enc. Bibl.*, 'Sihon.'

---

[1] See note 1 on p. 67.

to south, and from the 'eshed[1] or 'ashedoth, the slopes or cliffs above the Dead Sea in the west, to the Midbar or Wilderness on the east. Slopes are elsewhere associated with the Midbar as among the principal features of the country[2]; and the particular 'Ashdoth-of-Pisgah shows that all the western wall of Moab was called the Slopes.

The next group of poems are the Redes or Oracles attributed to Balaam, a prophet from beyond Israel; and they occur in the course of the narrative of his employment by Balak, king of Moab. Alarmed by Israel's defeat of Sihon, Balak sent for Balaam to ban this people which threatened to eat up all the rest. But by the influence of Israel's God Balaam refused to curse, and blessed Israel, acknowledging their irresistibleness under divine guidance and predicting their dominion over their neighbours. The structure of the narrative, the language and slight historical reflections of the oracles, the relations of these poems to one another and to their prose context, start questions which it would take a whole lecture to follow. I can deal with them only so far as to illustrate our present theme.[3]

The prose narrative is one of the finest in the Old Testament. Partly from the language, partly from inconsistencies among the things told, it is clear that the writer has used two different traditions of the story and worked them with some changes into the finished form which excites our admiration. His indifference to certain discrepancies of detail is the indifference of a powerfully dramatic and ethical spirit absorbed in representing the conflict of rival religious influences and the victory, even in a heathen mind, of that purer and more potential cause with which Israel was identified. Our interest in so lofty an issue is not disturbed by the facts that Balaam is described now as an Aramean from as far away as the Euphrates, and again as an Ammonite riding on his ass from the immediately neighbouring province; now as convoyed by the princes of Balak, and again as accompanied by only two servants; now as receiving God's permission to go to Balak, and again as exciting God's wrath by going. Indeed, the last of these differences may be due, not to two

[1] So we might read instead of the Heb. 'ªsher pointed as doubtful by the Massoretes themselves.

[2] Joshua xii. 8 (cf. x. 40).

[3] The English student will find an admirable analysis and criticism of prose and poetry in G. B. Gray's commentary (pp. 307 ff.) in the *International Critical Commentary* (T. & T. Clark), and should consult besides Addis, *Documents of the Hexateuch*, vol. i; Carpenter and Harford-Battersby, *The Hexateuch*; Foster Kent, *The Beginnings of Hebrew History*. In German see Holzinger's Commentary or the notes and introduction to his translation of the passage in Kautzsch's *Die Heilige Schrift des A.T.*

distinct traditions, but to the naïve effort of one and the same narrator to convey the first confused effects upon Balaam's mind of a religious force higher than the spirit in which he was accustomed to perform his offices. Such an ambiguity would be natural in a man dazzled by his encounter with a new light, and the narrator would but follow the method of his age by articulating the ambiguity into opposite commands from God. This is, however, a subsidiary point, and does not affect our reading of the writer's treatment of the mind and character of Balaam. In Balaam himself the writer is interested throughout. Recently this interest has been ignored, as if Balaam's character did not matter much in the development of the drama, or has even been explicitly denied.[1] It is true that the religious interests of the story dominate the psychological. The main issue is between the irresistible purpose of God with Israel and the human powers which from Pharaoh to Balak have sought to frustrate it. But this conflict is described—in detail and with zest—as being waged and issuing to an assurance of Israel's prosperity within the experience and the conduct of Balaam himself. I sympathize, therefore, with the older expositors who have concentrated their attention upon Balaam's behaviour; only I agree that some of them have taken the wrong way with this. They have treated Balaam as the victim of avarice,[2] of which vice there is no imputation to him in the story. On the contrary, when Balak's promise of reward is repeated, Balaam becomes only the more decided not to disobey the Word of God. There is a conflict in his mind, but it is not between obedience to God and avarice or ambition. It is of a more interesting kind from an historical point of view: a conflict between the customs and ideas with which the seers of the heathen Semites usually worked, and the new religious influence of a higher order which is represented as coming upon him from Israel's God. The issue is between that God and the religions of the time, and it is worked out in the experience of one of their prophets.

Balaam is essentially an Arab kāhin or seer of that early type, which combined the priest's offices of ritual, the diviner's reliance on omens and lots, and the prophet's experience of ecstasy and dreams. Some of these men rose to great fame in Arabia, and were often called, as Balaam was called by Balak, from a great distance by tribal chiefs when in difficulties.[3] As we have seen, one of the

[1] The latter by Prof. G. B. Gray on p. 318 of his Commentary.

[2] For example, Bishop Butler, *Sermon* vii. Newman, on the contrary, says (*Parochial and Plain Sermons*, iv, p. 122) that Balaam 'did not make up his mind for himself according to the suggestions of avarice or ambition'.

[3] Wellhausen, *Reste des Arab. Heidentums*, 131.

principal functions for which they were paid was to curse the foes of their employers in the name of God; and this might naturally be done to the accompaniment of sacrifices and other religious rites, and by the reading of omens or the casting of lots. To these practices the narrative represents Balaam as accustomed [1]; and up to the end of Balak's efforts to get him to curse Israel, and to change his message by changing his site (a characteristically Pagan resource), it is Balaam himself who directs the building of altars and the preparation of sacrifices. But while continuing to try these, his professional rites and shifts, he holds true to one thing—that he will only speak the word which *God shall speak* to him. In modern terms this is just to set a man's personal conviction, which he believes to be inspired by God, against the religious customs and conceptions of his time, his duty to his employer, and (if you like) his own prejudices and interests. All the influences of the life to which Balaam belonged, all the traditions of his office, and the power of the king who engaged him were opposed to the line that he took from first to last in obedience to what he believed to be the voice of God. Nor is our appreciation of the quality of his prophecy to be lessened by the fact that he did not rise clear of the passion of the primitive seer, but is described as working under ecstasy or in a trance. In Israel, the beginnings of the new and higher order of prophecy were in ecstasy; and uncontrollable excitement, to the pitch of utter insensibility to the material world, has characterized the origins of genuinely religious movements within Christianity itself. The man has the servile temper which does not understand the fullness of the truth that is come to him and staggers beneath the burden of it; but all the same this inspires him to rebel against the conventions and prejudices of his day and to overcome them. Balaam grovelled under his convictions, but he honestly uttered them. So, too, Mohammed behaved beneath the strength of his earliest revelations; but he lived to bring the whole of Arabia to his feet. For this is the spirit which, though fallen and blinded as Balaam describes himself to be, God shall one day call to stand up, and shall send upon its way in full control of its faculties. This is the spirit which, because it has been true as a slave, shall at last hear the glad words: Henceforth I call you not slaves but friends; for the slave knoweth not what his lord doeth, but I have called you friends, for all things that I have heard of my Father I have made known to you. In Balaam we have the one end

[1] xxiv. 1. *He went not, as from time to time, to meet omens.* The subordinate clause may either mean *as previously* (but the narrator has preserved no notice of this from his sources) or *as usually*.

of that long course of gradual revelation of which the other is reached in Christ and His disciples.

For in early Israel we see Prophecy so clearly rising out of the same religious environment, and by means of the same personal convictions of inspiration, that the experience of Balaam may well stand for a symbol of its origins. The earliest Hebrew seers, like those among their Arab kinsmen, were entrusted with the conduct of the primitive religious ritual common to all Semites, with divination by omens and lot-craft, with blessing the arms of their people and banning their foes, with the finding of lost property and the detection of criminals; and the trance and the dream were also their regular means of discovering the divine will, and of baptism to its service. But gradually all these things were discarded by the prophets of Israel. Under Samuel, Prophecy is separated from the national ritual, with its superstitious and paralysing effects. From Samuel's time onwards, Prophecy repudiates divination, necromancy and traffic with spirits or *jinns*. With men like Elijah, Micaiah-ben-Imlah, and Amos it throws off allegiance to political patrons, and by individual experience and conviction separates itself —very explicitly in the case of Amos—from the profession which bears its name. In time it rises free even of ecstasy, and as St. Paul says, the spirits of the prophets became subject to the prophets. The temper of these revolts and renunciations, which mark the rise of prophecy in Israel, appears in the prime of prophecy as a moral hostility to, and an intellectual scorn of, ritual, magic, ecstasy, the political ambitions of the kings and the unethical ideals of the people; all upon the strength of personal convictions which the great prophets ascribe, as simply as Balaam does, to the word of God. To the last the distinction of the true prophets from the false is based on the force of character with which they stood loyal to this word and refused all compromises with its demands.

Such analogies between the story of Balaam and the rise of prophecy in the early kingdom of Israel suggest that the period of the latter was also that in which Balaam's story grew to its present form. The atmosphere of both the prose and the verse is agreeable to this inference: it is an atmosphere of national confidence and rich in the instincts of growth.[1] The period of the early kingdom is also that to which modern criticism has reasonably assigned the composition of the two documents of the Hexateuch[2]—however much older some of their contents may be—out of which the narrative has been woven.

[1] G. B. Gray takes this as the strongest point in the argument for an early date.
[2] The Yahwist and Elohist.

Some allusions in the poems point in the same direction. Israel has already a king[1] and the kingdom is not yet divided. In the third oracle the mention of Agag suggests a date not distant from the reign of Saul; the Samaritan and some Greek versions substitute Gog for Agag, but if 'Agag' was not the original reading it is hard to see why a later scribe hit upon it for insertion in a poem assigned to a date before Saul. On the other hand, 'Gog' would be a very natural substitute to a later generation for the now forgotten or irrelevant 'Agag'. The only king described as effecting the conquest both of Moab and Edom, celebrated in the fourth oracle, was David; but the text of this allusion is uncertain. In spite of the uncertainty of some of these details in the evidence, the convergence of them all is impressive, and I therefore feel it to be very probable that the poems were composed between the time of Saul and that of the disruption of the kingdom. It is possible that they are founded upon shorter oracles handed down under Balaam's name; but of this there is no proof, and no allusion appears to Sihon or the events immediately leading up to the situation on which Balaam acts. The argument that some of the words and phrases are late and that those which are old are artificial archaisms is inconclusive.[2] It is accompanied by an interpretation of certain passages as Messianic and eschatological,[3] which appears to me forced. The temper and situation reflected by the poetry, their agreement with Arab feelings and customs, and in fact the whole incidence of the religious conflict celebrated do not even faintly suggest post-exilic conditions; but, as I have argued, they are suitable to those of the early kingdom. Some lines may of course be later additions.

The measure is normally of 3 stresses to the line; but there are such irregularities as by this time we have learned to expect, and some lines have 4, others not more than 2. The lines are in couplets,

[1] xxiv. 7, 17.

[2] For example it seems to me very precarious to conclude that words like shur, to view, and za'am, to damn, are evidence of a late date *for verse* because elsewhere they appear only in later writings. Za'am indeed is a common Semitic root and in Arabic has sometimes the force of a solemn assertion in discommending or traducing a person. The reduplicated forms harᵉrē and lᵉbadad may have been used for metrical reasons from an early date. There is no necessity to take tᵉru'ah in its post-exilic sense of a jubilant cry: it may mean war-cry or challenge or, more vaguely, sound. Nor even are the parallels Ya'ᵃḳob-Isra'el, Yahweh-'El, 'awen-'amal improbable in early poetry: see p. 95. Other terms prominent in the poems occur in J and E; and as noted above there are certain archaic forms of words. The argument that the language of the poems is late and also that the poems are to be interpreted as Messianic is that of von Gall, *Zusammensetzung und Herkunft der Bileam-Perikope* (1900).

[3] e. g. the allusions to a king and even the last couplet of xxiii. 9.

the parallelism of which is very regular. In fact these oracles of Balaam illustrate more fully than any other of our poems the various forms of Hebrew parallelism. The only third or odd lines occur in the third and fourth oracles, xxiv. 4, 8, and 18, where the text is uncertain. The greater regularity of the verse points, in harmony with the above arguments, to a date later than the Song of Deborah.

Each oracle is introduced by the formula: And he lifted his mashál and said.

The first Rede or Oracle of Balaam is xxiii. 7–10,

7. From 'ᴬrám Balák̦ doth bring me,
Mo'áb's king from hills of the East:
'Go curse me Ya'ᵃk̦ób,
And go damn Isra'el.'
8. How curse I, whom God curseth not,
And how damn Yahwéh hath not damned.
9. For from the rocks'-head I see him,
And from the heights I behold him.
Lo, a people dwelling alone,
Nor reckons itself with the nations.
10. Who hath measured the dust of Ya'ᵃk̦ób,
Or counted Isra'el's myriads?
May I die the death of the upright,
And like his be my end!

The second Rede or Oracle is in xxiii. 18–24.

18. Arise, Balák̦ and hearken,
Give ear to me, son of Ṣippór!
19. God is not man to belie,
Nor man's son to repent.
Hath He said, and doth not perform,
Or spoken and will not fulfil it?
20. Behold, to bless I have gotten,
And, blessing, I will not reverse it.
21. I mark nothing wrong with Ya'ᵃk̦ób,
Nor spy any strain on Isra'él;
Yahwéh, his God is with him,
And the noise of a King is upon him.

7. For 'ᴬram some propose 'ᴱdom, but the East is no unsuitable parallel for 'ᴬram. In the next couplets three verbs are used: 'arar, za'am and k̦abab, all onomatopoeic. The last two are found with analogous meanings in Arabic and are imitations of the angry braying or grunting of the camel. But the Arabic derivatives of K̦abab suggest that it meant originally to speak with a hollow voice—ventriloquially; it was therefore applicable to the utterers of spells, as here.

10. The second line is given above after the Samaritan and Gk. versions. Heb. Or the tale of the fourth of 'Isra'el. The connection of the last couplet with the foretext is far to seek, and many take it as the addition of a later scribe.

20. Blessing, or with Sam. and Gk., I will bless.

21. I mark, so Sam., &c.; Heb. He, or one, marks. King, i.e. God, as the parallel shows, and not a human king.

22. 'Tis God out of Egypt that brings him,
And his is the strength (?) of the wild-ox.
23. For magic is not in Ya'ᵃḳób,
Nor lot-craft in Isra'él;
But duly 't is told to Ya'ᵃḳób,
To Isra'el, what God hath wrought.
24. Lo, the folk like a lioness riseth,
And like to a lion uprears;
Nor will couch till he eateth the prey,
And drinketh the blood of the slain.

The third Rede or Oracle is in xxiv. 3–9.

3. Rede of Bil'ám, Bᵉ'ór's-son,
And rede of the eye-sealed (?) man,
4. [Who heareth the speech of God]
In vision seeth Shaddái,
Falling, yet open of eye.
5. How goodly thy tents, Ya'ᵃḳób,
Thy dwellings, Isra'el!
6. Like valleys they spread,
Like riverside gardens,
Like cedars God planted,
Like oaks (?) upon water.
7. Streams water from 's buckets, (?)
His seed 's on great waters, (?)!

22. Strength (?). The word is obscure: others translate swiftness, others horns.

23. See G. B. Gray, who takes the meaning given above to the second couplet as impossible, and the whole verse as interpolated. Others (e. g. Holzinger) translate the preposition attached in the first couplet to Jacob and to Israel as against, i. e. magic and lot-craft are of no use against these, and do not stick to them. The meaning is appropriate to the context. It is only a too rigorous and modern taste which rejects the next couplet on the grounds of metre. The translation, now must one say of Jacob and Israel, What hath God wrought? is possible and agreeable to Holzinger's translation of the previous couplet.

3, 4. Rede, nᵉ'um, the usual term used by Hebrew prophets of their oracles. Eye-sealed (?), if this be the meaning it refers to the trance or ecstasy into which the seer falls, physically his eyes are closed, and is in intentional paradox to the open of eye; with the inner eye he sees God. It was the custom of Mohammed when he felt his earlier revelations approaching to have himself wrapped up in order to receive them. Cf. the Ḳoran, Sura lxxiv, beginning 'O thou, the enwrapped one'. The first line of verse 4 disturbs the couplet-form and is probably an interpolation from verse 16, where it has a parallel. If we are to retain it here, we must restore that parallel.

6. Valleys, wadies, or torrent-beds which even when dry (especially on the east of Jordan) display long stretches of colour, green and purple, with the oleanders (Rose-bay, Rose-laurel) and other bushes that fill them. The analogy here lies in the extent of the flourishing aspect and its hidden sources. Cedars, oaks (?), the two tree-names are transposed from their positions in the Heb. text (Cheyne and others), as cedars are not found on waters. Oaks is substituted, as by many, for the doubtful Heb. for aloes.

7. The text is uncertain. The first couplet as it stands celebrates either as in

Higher is his king than 'Agág
And lifted his kingdom.
8a. 'Tis God out of Egypt that brings him,
And his is the strength of the wild-ox.
9a. He hath crouched, hath couched like a lion,
Like a lioness who shall rouse him?
8b. Let him eat the nations his foes,
And their bones let him crunch!
[Shatter his oppressors?]
9b. Who bless thee be blesséd,
And curséd who curse thee.

The fourth Rede or Oracle is in xxiv. 15–19.

15. Rede of Bil'ám, Be'ór's-son,
And rede of the eye-sealed (?) man,
16. Who heareth the speech of God,
And knows what the Highest doth know;
In vision he seeth Shaddaí,
Falling, yet open of eye.
17. I see him—but not now,
I descry him—but not near.
A star has gone up from Ya'aḳób,
A sceptre from Isra'el rises,
And shatters the brows of Mo'áb,
The skulls of all sons of Sheth (?).
18. And 'Edóm shall be dispossessed,
And dispossessed be Se'ir;
While Isra'el gains in might,
And Ya'aḳób doth rule them, his foes (?)
[And the rest of Se'ir doth perish.]

similar Arabic figures the bounty of Israel or more probably the fertility of the people. But some emend the text so as to read, Let people tremble at his might—and his arm be on many nations.—For 'Agag, Gk. and Sam., read Gog, the synonym in later Israel for heathen power.

8, 9. I have, following others, transposed the last three lines of 8 and the first two of 9. The text of the former is uncertain; the triplet is suspicious, though not impossible (see above, p. 18). Some emend so as to give two lines, e.g. Volz: He eateth, he cruncheth his foes—their bones he shatters; and Holzinger: He shatters, he crunches his foes—he eats, he devours their bones.

15, 16. See on 3, 4. Heb. Knoweth the knowledge of the Highest, i.e. what the Highest knows. Cp. the words in the 'Throne-verse' in the Ḳoran: 'they comprehend nought of His knowledge.'

17. Gone up, darak, which in Arab. = to rise to the zenith, so perhaps here. Skulls, Sam. skull, cp. Jer. xlviii. 45. Heb. gives a verb: break down. Sheth (?); it is doubtful if this is a name, or means tumult or pride.

18. Text uncertain. His foes stands at the end of line two, and gives it an accent too many; while line four has an accent too few. I have transferred it to the latter. The fifth line breaks the prevailing order of couplets, but coming at the end and as a climax is not impossible (see above, p. 20). Se'ir, so by changing one letter I propose to read instead of Me'ir of the city. For other reconstructions see the commentaries.

There follow three shorter Redes, xxiv. 20–24, which are generally, and with reason, held to be of later origin than the four preceding. The first on the Arabs south of the Negeb: And he saw ' maleḳ and raised his mashál and said:

20. First of nations 'Amaléḳ,
But his end is to perish.

The second on the Arab Kenites: And he saw the Ḳenite and raised his mashál and said:

21. Lasting thy seat, Ḳaín,
Fast to the rock thine eyrie;
22. But yet it is to be burned,—
Till when? 'Ashúr shall enthral thee.

The third, according to the Greek version, is upon Gog: And he saw Gog and raised his mashál and said:

23. Coasts shall . . . from the north,
24. And ships from beside Kittím,
And afflict 'Ashúr, É'ber afflict,
And he in his turn is to perish.

With the conquest of Northern Moab and Gilead, and the conquest—perhaps in many cases the peaceful appropriation—of the hill-country of western Palestine, Israel suffered the social and economic changes which I described in last lecture.[1] They ceased to be desert tribes, more or less nomadic, and settled in villages and fortified towns to the cultivation of fields and orchards. The process of change is very finely described in a poem which, though it comes next in order in our series, certainly in part and probably in whole belongs at earliest to the very end of our period; for it reflects the troubles which fell on the nation, and implies as imminent, if not actual, their exile. It is the long ode ascribed to Moses in Deutero-

20. First, usually taken as of quality; the antithesis end proves it to be of time.

21. Ḳain, transferred to this line, which is a stress short, from the next, which has one too many. Thine eyrie, Heb. Ḳinnekha, a play upon the name Ḳain.

21. The first line is thus in the text: 'Ôi mi yiḥyeh missŭmo'el which can be translated, Ah who shall live after God appoints him, i.e. to death. But by a slight alteration of consonants and vowels we get 'iîm . . . miss^{e}m'ol (or coasts . . . from the north or northwards); and coasts stand in parallel in the later prophets to ships (or to them that go down into the sea), Isa. xlii. 10, lx. 9; and are mentioned with Kittim (Cyprus). They are frequently personified and stand for their inhabitants; but what the verb is to which they are the nominative here, I cannot say. Compare 'the king of the north with many ships' in Dan. xi. 40, also x. 30. 'Ashur and 'Eber = Across, i.e. the Euphrates, are synonymous. For other, to the present writer, less probable reconstructions, see the commentaries.

[1] pp. 29, 30.

nomy xxxii. The metre is in couplets of normally three stresses to the line, but the glorious swing of it cannot be rendered in English by a strict adherence to the rule. Indeed there are the usual irregularities. Some lines, generally, be it observed, in climax to a phase of the song, have four stresses—

7. Remember the days of yore,
Scan the years, age upon age.
Ask of thy sire to acquaint thee,
Thine elders that they may tell thee:—
8. When the Highest gave nations their heritage,
When He sundered the children of men,
The bounds of the peoples He set
By the tale of the sons of Isra'el.
9. For the lot of Yahwéh is His folk,
And Ya'akób the scale of His heritage.
10. In a land of the desert He found him,
In the void and the howl of the waste.
He cast around him, He scanned him,
As the pupil of His eye He watched him.
11. As an eagle stirreth his nest,
Fluttereth over his young,
Spreadeth his wings, receives them,
Lifteth them up on his pinions;
12. Yahwéh alone was his leader
And never a strange god with Him.
13. The highlands He gave him to ride,
And to feed from the growth of the hills.
Suckled him with honey from crags,
And oil from the flint of the rocks.
14. Curd of the kine, milk of the sheep,
With the fat of the lambs,

8. Gave . . . heritage: caused them to inherit, enfeuded them, to use an old law term.

Sons of Isra'el. Two Gk. versions—sons of God.

10. Void, both tracklessness and emptiness: tohu, one of the two terms for chaos. Cast around: more probably encircled or circled around him than surrounded him. Pupil, happier than the A.V. apple. Heb. is 'īshōn (for inshon) and Arabic 'insān, little man, the tiny image reflected in the centre of the eye. Discerned, carefully or anxiously considered him, kept his eye on him.

11. Eagle or vulture of the desert. His, the father-bird, not her as in A.V.

13. Hills, sadi or sadeh, apparently in this earlier sense of the word, and not field: thus parallel to highlands or heights and suitable to Israel's settlement on a mountain-range. Oil . . . rocks. Of course, not rock or mineral oil; but the oil of the olive, which never yields oil so richly as when planted on rocky limestone terraces. In alluvial soil the tree's berries are less rich.

14. The beeves of Bashan were also celebrated for their size; he-goats, 'athudim, in Heb. only here; but also in Arabic. Kernels, Heb. kidneys. The last line is one of the finest specimens of a climax in a 'swell-verse' that we have met with.

Rams of Bashán's-breed and goats
With the fat of the kernels of wheat;
And the blood of the grape thou drankest in foam!

The origin which we have ventured to describe for Israel could not be more vividly confirmed: a 'clatch' of desert eaglets, that might have remained in the desert for ever but for the impulse and guidance of their God, who guarded them from the dangers of the trackless wilderness and brought them to the fertile ranges of Palestine. The great prophets paint similar pictures, but like this ode with gloomy issues: Hosea, when he describes Israel's idyllic life with Yahweh alone in the desert, and her wooing of other gods after she reached the corn and wine and flax and wool to which He brought her; and Jeremiah in one of the finest of his earlier lyrics [1]:

For thee I recall the troth of thy youth,
  The love of thy bridals,
Thy following of Me in the desert,
  The land not sown!
Holy Isra'el to Yahwéh,
  First-fruits of His income!
Who bit [2] him were doomed all,
  Evil fell on them.

He then contrasts the very different experience of his own times when Israel was the prey of every nation.

But our deliberate ode, though it also will travel as far, has not done so yet. In equally beautiful verse it describes the change to the fertile ranges of Palestine. Nine packed lines give the material blessings to which these desert nomads have been brought by God: plateaus and hill-sides covered with corn, olives and honey; larger, richer breeds of cattle than the desert bears; fat wheat, and for a climax the enjoyment of wine. This is reserved for the last line—the ninth wave—a 'swell-verse', heavier and longer than the others.

The same gift is described more lavishly in 'the Blessing of Jacob' on Judah, Gen. xlix; and the lavishness is confirmed by the remains of ancient vineyards still apparent on his land, and by the reports of early travellers before the Moslem rule diminished the culture of the vine in Judah:

11. Binding his foal to the vine,
  To the choice vine his she-ass' colt,

[1] Ch. ii. 2, 3.

[2] Or ate of: the verb is used in continuation of the metaphor that Israel were first-fruits of Yahweh; but we may note that the Arabs have a similar figure quoted by Musil, *Ethnolog. Bericht*, 345, in the complaint of an Arab against 'my kinsman who eateth my right', 'ibn 'ammī makel ḥaḳḳi.

He washes his raiment in wine,
In the blood of the grape his apparel;
12. Dim are his eyes with wine,
And white his teeth with milk.

Other verses in the same blessing describe other features of the land's fertility:

15. He saw the rest, it was good,
And the land how fair!
22. A fruitful branch is Yoséph,
Fruitful branch by a well,
The twigs run over the wall.
25. Blessings of heaven above,
Blessings of the deep beneath,
Blessings of breasts and womb.

Or these lines from the other edition of the Blessing in Deut. xxxiii:

13. And of Yoseph he said:
Blessed of Yahwéh is his land,
With the bloom of heaven above,
And the deep that crouches beneath,
14. With the bloom of the fruits of the sun,
The bloom of the pulse of the moons,
15. The tops of the ancient heights,
And the bloom of the hills of old.
16. With the bloom of the land and its fullness,
And His grace Who dwelt in the bush.

24. And of Asher he said:
Most blessed of sons Ashér,
Of his brothers most favoured,
He dippeth his foot in oil.

Or the conclusion:

28. And Isra'el dwells in peace,
Secluded the fount of Ya'ᵃḳób,
In a land of corn and wine,
His heavens, too, dropping the dew.

We have seen that Arab poetry shows few reflections of trade; so too the early poetry of Israel. The infrequent references to commerce are faint and even doubtful. They all occur in the poems from which the last quotations are made: Gen. xlix.—

13. Zᵉbŭlún dwelleth on the shore of the sea,
And is for an haven of ships,
With his flank on Ṣidón.

And Issachar:

14. He stoops his shoulder to carry,
Becomes a servant for hire.

And the parallel in Deut. xxxiii:

18. Rejoice Zᵉbŭlún in thine issues,
In thy tents 'Issachár!
They call the tribes to the hill,
There slay the offerings due.
Yea, the wealth of the seas they suck,
The hidden hordes of the sand.

These tribes, settled in neighbourhood to the Phoenicians, could not be kept from trade. The last two couplets appear to describe that combination of worship and commerce at religious festivals, which was characteristic of the whole Semitic world, and was illustrated alike at Mecca, at Sinai, at Jerusalem and Bethel, and at Hierapolis on the Euphrates.

In the narratives of the conquest of Western Palestine only two poetical pieces are quoted, the fragment addressed by Joshua to the sun and moon (Joshua x. 12, 13), and the long Ode or Song of Deborah (Judges v).

The former, you remember, is introduced thus: the people of Gibeon, on the back of the central range, were besieged by Amorites jealous of their treaty with Israel, and sent to Joshua for help. Joshua came up from Gilgal by night, took the Amorites by surprise, and chased them over the range to its western slopes by the two Beth-horons. Then spake Joshua to Yahweh, and in the face of Israel said:

O Sun, on Gib'ón be thou still,
And Moon, on the vale 'Ayyalón.
The Sun is still, and the Moon hath stood,
Till the folk be avenged on their foes.

Both these couplets are given as 'written in the Book of Yashar'.[1] But the second of them has its difficulties. It cannot be scanned in the measure of the first which has three stresses to the line; and the first line of it may be read as a statement that the preceding prayer of Joshua has been fulfilled: 'so the sun was still and the moon did stand.' Such a record, however, Joshua could not have uttered at that moment, nor till the day was over. Some,[2] therefore, take the line as a prose gloss on the verse, and read this as a triplet. But such a gloss, of exactly the same meaning as the note which the narrator immediately hastens to give, is improbable, and the line has not only a poetical syntax,[3] but scans with four stresses, just as its successor does. We must, therefore, take it as part of the poem, but in Joshua's mouth at

[1] Above, Introduction.
[2] Wellhausen and Budde.
[3] Moon is anarthrous and precedes its verb.

the very moment he has uttered the prayer; its verbs must be understood not in the past but in the present,[1] as is rendered above.

The fragment, then, is a prayer, and the confident expression of its fulfilment—a prayer for the day to last long enough for the full rout of Israel's foes. But after quoting it from the Book of Yashar, the narrator gives its poetical expression a prose interpretation, and says that 'the sun stood in the centre of the heavens and did not press to set about a whole day'. The miracle which he assumes (but which is not asserted by his quotation) he takes as having happened at noon. But the relative positions given by the verse to sun and moon—over Gibeon and over Ayyalon—are possible only in the early morning. They are perfectly suitable to Joshua's standpoint if, as the narrative implies, he surprised the Amorites just at dawn, and in the pursuit of them reached the descent by the Beth-horons two or three hours after sunrise. There is no reason to doubt that this poem, like so many others, is the tradition of an actual event, but it does not suggest that this event was a miracle.

The Song or Ode of Deborah not only reflects the various positions of the tribes after the settlement and the struggles with the Canaanites through which they won, and after repeated shocks held to, these; but it betrays as well the temptations by which the varied surface of their new country enticed some of them to sacrifice the national interests to their own economic advantage. On this a few notes are necessary.

If the tradition of the prophets is true, that Israel upon their migration from Egypt were already a national unity, consisting of all the twelve tribes who were afterwards comprised under the national name, that unity was gravely imperilled, if not destroyed, by the conditions of their settlement in Palestine. The tribal territories were not only separated by natural and political barriers, but in the various qualities of their soils impressed their inhabitants with different ideals of life, or by their positions towards the rest of the world opened to them different lines of culture. The mountain ranges, on which the Israelites settled, are divided from each other by the deep Jordan valley and the broad plain of Esdraelon, both at that time still held by the Canaanites.[2] Nor were the mountains free. A belt of towns retained by the enemy—Gezer, Ayyalon, Shaalbim and Jerusalem, with perhaps Gibeon, Chephirah, Beeroth and Kiriath-Yearim[3]—lay

[1] Their forms, the equivalent of a perfect, and a pure perfect, are quite agreeable to such a rendering, and often occur in this sense in a prayer or a prophecy.

[2] Judges i. 27; Joshua xvii. 11, 12.

[3] Judges i. 21, 29, 35; Joshua ix. 17, xv. 63, xvi. 10.

right across the western range, and cut off Judah and Simeon to the south. Reuben and Gad were settled on the east of Jordan, where man's wealth consists mainly in sheep and cattle. On the west, Ephraim and Manasseh succeeded to fields and orchards as rich as any in Syria; while Benjamin's and Judah's lands, though suitable for the vine and olive, were rocky and ran into desert. Asher and Naphtali shared their fertile soil with numerous *enclaves* of Canaanite peasants, while Asher, Zebulun and Issachar touched the sea-coast and the trading centres of Phoenicia; and even Dan in his nook under Mount Hermon heard the call of the sea and its ships. Thus divided both by nature and culture, the tribes grew callous to their common interests, lost not only the physical strength but the moral spirit and order of union, and fell a prey to the jealous reactions of the peoples whom they had dispossessed.

It is such conditions, and such a crisis, that the Song of Deborah reflects—reflects, but only to sing of how Israel overcame them through the faith and eloquence of a few individuals who, in enthusiasm for the national God, rallied several of the tribes to war and led them to a victory over the Canaanites upon the plain of Esdraelon. That the two chief leaders to this victory, Deborah and Barak, are represented as the singers of the Song, and that one of them was a woman, will not surprise us after what we have learned of the authorship of songs of war—and songs of the passions of praise and of satire—among Israel's kinsmen the Arabs.[1] The contemporary character of the Song is clear, and is generally recognized: it can be denied only by ignoring the evidence of the language and perverting that of the substance and spirit of the poetry. The language has no late features, except possibly in verses 2, 3.[2] There are none of those reflections of subsequent facts and conditions which appear in the Song of Moses. The situation of the time is faithfully rendered; no late writer would have omitted all notice of Judah, but must have mentioned that tribe either for praise or blame. Also Manasseh or Machir is still west of the Jordan. Most conclusive, however, are the force and passion of the poetry; in a people of the Semitic type of imagination it is very doubtful whether so natural, so vivid, and so convincing a representation of the events could have been achieved except under the immediate impressions of them.[3] The very corruptions and obscurities of the text, due to long oral tradition, support the rest of the evidence. The undoubted irregularities in the metre show a more primitive style than either the Song of Moses or Balaam's

[1] Above, pp. 30, 36–38.

[2] See Budde's note on these verses.

[3] See above, pp. 36, 37.

oracles. Whoever was its author, the Song springs to us from the heart of the time.

But there is just as little reason to doubt that the author was Deborah herself. This has been denied on the grounds that the poem speaks both of Deborah and Barak in the third person (verse 15), and addresses them in the second (12); and that the form of the verb in the phrase (7) 'Till *I*, Deborah, arose', may also be spelt, 'Till *thou* didst arise.' None of these things, however, is incompatible with the authorship of Deborah, which, in the first place, is shown to be probable from the fact that similar songs are frequently the work of women among the Arabs, and secondly, is assured by the character and temper of certain parts of this one. The changes of measure, as well as the abrupt changes of subject or point of view which coincide with them, have been taken as implying more than one author; and they might be read, of course, as corroborative of the double authorship ascribed to the Song—its ascription to Barak as well as Deborah. But there can be little doubt to whom we should assign the verses on Jael and on the mother of Sisera. If Deborah did not make them, some other woman did.

The names Barak and Deborah belong to a primitive type of Hebrew names unconnected with that of the national God. Barak means Lightning, and occurs elsewhere in the Semitic world, notably as the name of the father of Hamilcar the Carthaginian; Deborah is the Hebrew word for Bee. What may have been the motive for such a name, when all personal names were still significant, can only be conjectured. There are several possibilities. 'Bee' may be derived from a family totem, or, as still happens among the Semites, from some accident or omen connected with the girl's birth. But as the name is given here to a prophetess and elsewhere to another tribal heroine, the nurse of Rachel, it may be a Hebrew parallel to the Greek Melissa, which was not only an epithet applied to poets, but the title of the Delphian prophetess and of other 'humming priestesses' of such prophetic deities as Demeter, her daughter and Cybele.[1] It is remarkable that the poem should contain what seems an intentional play upon the name Deborah in the verb dabberi 'utter' or 'speak'.[2]

[1] Prof. W. R. Smith, *Journal of Philology*, xiv, p. 120, who refers also to the tree or palm-tree of Deborah and points out that 'the tree of the bee' is parallel to the 'tree of the soothsayers who hum or murmur hoarsely', me'onenim. For the questions raised by the tree of Deborah, referred to our prophetess in Judges iv, and by the nurse of Rachel who was buried in the same neighbourhood, see the commentaries.

[2] Verse 12. All this suggests another derivation for dibber, to speak, than that suggested above, Lecture I, p. 9, *n.* 2; as if the word were onomatopoeic and meant

But all this is uncertain. It is quite possible that a female child was called the Bee in the hope that she would prove a diligent worker and good manager.[1] For whatever reason our Deborah received the name, she lived to deserve it. She had a governing instinct for the order which she emphasizes, and proved a queen-bee in Israel's hive when many of the men were drones; nor was she without her sting.

Like others of our poems, the Song opens with praise to God and with a call for listeners, probably in this case the chiefs of the tribes whom Israel fought (verses 2, 3); and then, like them also, describes a Theophany in the usual form of a thunderstorm, not that which took place on Sinai at the giving of the law, but Yahweh marches from His dwelling on the mountains of the south to help His people in this fresh crisis (4, 5). Then follows a picture of the weakness and disorder in Israel before Deborah arose a mother in Israel (6–8); then the inspiration of the new leaders and the readiness of the people (9–12), and the rally to war of six of the tribes, Benjamin, Ephraim, and Manasseh from the south; Issachar, Zebulun, and Naphtali from the north (11 c, 13–15), with whom are satirically contrasted the laggard Reuben, Gad, Dan and Asher (15 c, 18). As has been already remarked, Judah (with Simeon ?) is not mentioned, shut off in the far south behind the Canaanite barrier. A brief chant follows on the battle itself, and mainly on its last rush in which the rain-storm, the thunder-clouds ridden by Yahweh, complete the discomfiture of the foe (19–22). Then comes a curse on the unknown Meroz (23), and the poem closes with its masterpiece, the wonderful passages contrasting Ya'el and her murder of Sis^{e}ra (24–27) with Sis^{e}ra's mother whining for his return and greedily expecting the spoil of the perished chief (28–30). A couplet has been added for epilogue, probably by a later hand.[2]

In parts the text is very bad, but only in parts. The early versions help us to repair it, but only sometimes, for the most of the corruptions are earlier than they, and sometimes they assist the meaning.

The dialect is apparently that of the northern tribes, with which Barak and Deborah are identified. It is flavoured with Aramaic; but

originally to murmur, then applied both to human speech, including the murmur of oracles, and to the bee, the humming or speaking insect; and that its application in several Semitic tongues to the herding of cattle came later: 'calling' the cattle.

[1] See the Greek addition to the text of the passage on the sluggard in Proverbs vi.

[2] Modern Literature on the Song: *National-Gesänge der Hebräer*, by Dr. K. W. Justi, 1816, an extraordinarily instructive work considering its date; the monograph by Rev. G. A. (now Professor) Cooke, of Oxford, *The History and Song of Deborah*, Judges iv and v (1892); G. F. Moore, 'Judges' (1895), in the *International Critical Commentary*; Karl Budde, 'Das Buch der Richter' (1895) in the *Kurzer Hand-Kommentar zum A.T.*

again, as in other poems, we find a number of words used in the same sense as in Arabic. There are also some features in the syntax which it is natural to regard as primitive; they do not occur elsewhere in the same meaning as here.[1]

The following account of the metres must be read under the impression of what has been said of the state of the text: bad in parts, but in parts only.

First we see plainly that parallelism was already in that early age the prevailing and dominant feature of Hebrew verse, but it is of the more free kind, as in other early and strong poems, and less artificial than it became in the latest verse. Remembering our rule,[2] we take it as the principal factor in dividing the lines. So divided these appear in a considerable variety of measure. For the most part this is of two or four stresses to the line; but there is also a considerable proportion of lines with three stresses; sometimes a Ḳinah couplet of 2 : 3, and sometimes a swell-line with five. The changes of metre sometimes coincide with a change of subject, that is, with the beginning of a new strophe, but sometimes happen within what is evidently the same strophe. On these latter we have three things to keep in mind; on the one hand the state of the text, on the other the probability that some irregularities were original to the metre, especially at so early an age, and that in reciting or singing they could be removed, as in the folk-songs of Palestine at the present day.[3] The metre of the opening strophes (verses 2–8) is nearly all of two stresses to the line, which seems to me to be the most primitive in Hebrew. Verses 9–12, describing the rise of the people's inspiration, have mostly three stresses to the line, but there are 2's and a 4. The rallying of the clans (11 c, 13–15) is chanted at first in 4's, but this breaks down before the end. The same measure prevails in the satire on the laggard tribes (15 c–18), but again with variations. The last couplet is 5 : 3. The rush of the battle itself (19–21) is mainly in 3's, and this measure seems to suit the subject. The quatrain on Meroz (23) has a measure to itself, 4 : 3, 4 : 3. Again, with the beginning of the passage on Ya'el (24–27) the measure changes to 3's, but swings between 3 and 4 with the character of the actions described. In the passage on Sisera's mother it settles again to 4's, except for the last lines, but here the text is difficult, and the measure may originally have been steady to the end. The epilogue is 4 : 4.

[1] e. g. the construction b^e . . . bar^{e}kū in the opening verse. For some well-known roots, e.g. ḥṣṣ (11), shrsh (14), gur (17), ḳedem (21), meanings are given not known elsewhere and apparent only from their context.

[2] Above, pp. 13, 17.

[3] See above, pp. 17, 18, &c.

Besides the textual uncertainties, there is the other usual difficulty of telling how many accents lay on the construct phrases. The Massoretes have pointed these differently, mostly leaving them without maḳḳeph, and therefore probably with two accents, but sometimes binding them with maḳḳeph, and so giving them one accent. This probably represents the usage throughout Hebrew history. In reciting or singing, the construct could be given with either one or two stresses to suit the rest of the line.[1] And this, above all, we must keep in mind: that the Song was to be sung or recited, not read. It may be right or wrong to do as I have done, and on the ground of the parallelism print groups of words under four stresses now as two lines and now as one. But as the song was for the ear, not the eye, this question does not matter. So too with the difficulties in the pronunciation of some single words, especially proper names. I am sure that Isra'el was often slurred into two syllables, and Mᵉgiddó in its line must be in two, just as we know an Arab can pronounce a name like Mkeis in one. In singing, the vocal sheva could be pronounced or omitted. The measure of some parallel lines shows that this must sometimes have been done.

There are no certain rhymes, but the reader will notice that the favourite position for sonorous proper names is the end of the line, and how often this is occupied by the name Isra'el, especially at the close of verses or strophes. Another point is the infrequent alliteration; for example, the double instance in 26. But there is more assonance.

All these peculiarities, and varieties, of the music I have sought to reproduce in the following translation, along with a literal rendering of the sense of the poem. But it is impossible to serve both ends perfectly, and I know I have often failed. In particular, some lines of Hebrew will not run into lines of English with the same number of stresses. What I offer is far less a final translation of the rhythm and the meaning than it is reliable material for this.

Then sang Deborah and Baraḳ ben-Abi-noʿam on that day saying:

2\. That leaders took lead in Isra'el,
That the people were willing,
Bless ye the Lord!

2, 3. Parallel lines of two stresses each (according to text which so gives the constructs) except the first, which may have three. Some translate line 1: For the loosing of locks in Israel, the loosing of the warriors' long hair in vow of war.

---

[1] A construct like ben-ʿAnáth, for instance, can only have had one accent.

3. Hearken, O kings,
Rulers give ear,
I to the Lord,
I am to sing,
I hymn the Lord,
God of Isra'el.

4. Lord at Thy start from Se'ir,
On Thy march from the mount of 'Edóm,
Earth did quake,
Heaven was swaying (?),
The clouds poured water,
5. The mountains streamed,
Before the Lord,
God of Isra'el.

6. In the days of Shamgár [ben-'Anáth]
Caravans ceased;
Who would be wayfaring
Fared by the byways.
7. Ceaséd had order (?),
In Isra'el it ceased;
Till I rose, Deboráh,
Rose mother in Isra'el.
8. Sacrifice ceased (?),
Barley-bread failed. (?)
Was shield seen or lance,
In the forty thousands of Isra'el?

The parallel in verse 9 supports the translation given above. Were willing, lit. freely offered themselves.

4, 5. The first and probably the second lines have three stresses each; so certainly the fifth; but the rest have two each. Only the text of the last four is very uncertain. Swaying: reading namoṭu, Heb. text nataphu, dropped or poured, as in the next line. Some Gk. recensions with ἐταράχθη and ἐξεστάθη suggest namoṭu or namogu, surge off, dissolve. Heb. adds This (is) Sinai, obviously an old gloss by one who thought that the theophany was that of the law-giving; and repeats Before the Lord, which if we retain renders the last line a 'swell', Streamed, Heb. nazelu; Gk. shook down, nazollu.

6, 7. The text adds in days of Ya'el, probably a gloss. Ben-'Anath also doubtful. The other lines of the two verses except the last have each two stresses. If ben-'Anath is retained the first couplet is a ḳinah, 3:2. For 'orohōth, roads, read 'orehoth, caravans. The second 'o. seems a dittography. Order or rule, or authority. So I render perazon on its obvious meaning in verse 11; others villages, peasantry, or agriculture. I rose, so the Heb. points; some point differently and in agreement with verse 12 read thou; some versions give she.

8. The reading of the first couplet is very uncertain. As given above the first line is a conjectural alteration of the text: they chose new gods, of which there is no trace in the Song. The second is based on the Greek. Seen, perhaps better shown, come to the light of day (Budde). So, already in 1816, Justi (*National-Gesänge der Hebräer*) 'es war nicht Schild zu sehen', &c.

9. My heart to the leaders in Isra'el,
To the willing of the people!
Bless ye the LORD!
10. Riding roan asses,
Sitting on carpets (?),
Walking the highway—sing (?) them!
11. Hark the huzzahing (?)
Where the herds water.
There are they telling the faith of the LORD,
Faith of His rule in Isra'el.

12. Rouse thee, rouse thee, Deboráh,
Rouse thee, [rouse thee,] deliver the song!
Arise, Barák,
Capture thy captors, ben-'Abi-no'ám!
11 c. [Then to the gates down came the LORD's folk,]
13. Then came down the rest of the great ones,
Down to the LORD came His folk with the brave ones,
14. Out of Ephráim they tore (?) to the valley,
After thee, Ben-yamin, with thy clans!

9. Metre as in verse 2. Leaders, ḥokekim: perhaps we should read meḥokekim as in verse 14, those who give commands: orderers. Willing, see verse 2.

10. A couplet 3:2; with a third line of 3. All classes of the people are called to give praise for the leaders or the willing of the people. Roan, ṣehoroth, reddish white. A form of the same root in Arabic, 'Aṣḥar is the name for an ass of a reddish colour; but other forms of the root are applied to the braying of the ass. Carpets is doubtful, but supported by the context; the Gk. has in judgement. Sing them, reading shīrum—the m being taken from the beginning of the next line where it is out of place; Heb. shiḥū[m], think upon them.

11. Huzzahing, Heb. meḥaṣeṣim, found only here; by some taken as a denom. from ḥeṣ, arrow, 'the archers'; by others from the Sem. root ḥaṣaṣ or ḥaṣi, gravel, 'the gravel-treaders.' The context shows that it has to do with sound or music, and so the Gk. takes it, 'those who strike up music.' Where the herds water, lit. among the draw-wells or watering troughs. Faith or good faith, Heb. ṣidḳōth, usually given in Eng. as righteousnesses, may as a plural mean deeds of good faith, by which Yahweh fulfils His promises; but is better taken for the singular. Rule, Heb. perazon, which others render peasantry; see above on verse 7.

12. Four lines, of 3, 3 [or 4], 2, 3. Note the assonance in Deboráh and dabberi, deliver or utter. The song, that is not the present song of triumph, but the previous song to beat up the tribes to battle (see above, pp. 37, 38). Some versions read the second line as: Arouse the myriads of the people. Captors, so Syr. and Ar. Heb. thy captives.

11 c, 13-15. The gathering of the clans. The measure changes to four stresses a line for six lines out of ten: the rest have three each.

11 c. Where it stands in the text (before 12) it seems out of place, both because it is an odd line there and has four stresses. Here it finds a fellow line of the same measure; but does not satisfactorily fit into the rhythm of couplets.

13. The two lines rhyme somewhat—'addīrīm, gibbōrīm.

14. Heb. Out of Ephraim their root in 'Amaleḳ. For the last word read 'emek, valley, with Gk. One Gk. reading also confirms root, but takes it

Out of Makhír came down commanders,
And from Z^{e}bulún the drawers of batons.
15. Naphtali's (?) lords with D^{e}boráh,
As Issakhár so was Barák,—
Into the valley shot at his heels!

In the septs of R^{e}'ubén great the heart-searchings!
16. Why satest thou still the wattles between?
To list to them whistling the flocks?
In the septs of R^{e}'ubén great the heart-searchings!
17. Gil^{e}'ád stayed at home over Jordan,
And Dan—why a truant in ships?
Ashér sat down on the shore of the sea,
And stayed by his creeks.
18. Z^{e}bulún—the tribe spurned life to the death,
With Naphtalí on the heights of the range.

as a verb (which the line also requires) with a suffix: ἐξερίζωσεν αὐτούς = uprooted them. If we accept some form of the root we get an idiom applied to rapid flight exactly the same as our Eng. tore. Others shullehu, were shot; or sharu, went. After thee, &c., confirmed by Gk. but difficult, possibly the slogan of Benjamin (with three stresses); the alternative is to take the line as addressed to Ephraim: Behind thee Ben-yamin among thy clans; or, with change of reading, his clans. Another Gk. reading gives thy brother, Ben-yamin. Makhir is Manasseh, still west of Jordan.

15. The text gives Issakhár in each of the first two lines. In the second Gk. has instead a second Barák. Both these repetitions are probably clerical errors, and most critics read Naphtali for the second Issakhar, but its more natural position is next to Z^{e}bulun in place of the first I. Shot, or let loose, Heb. shullaḥ, a passive. Heels, Heb. feet. The Gk. reading and division give us two last lines of four stresses each. This is the same rhythm as the rest and may be original:

And Issachar's lords with D^{e}boráh and Barák,
So Barak to the valley was shot on his feet (?).

15. Begins the satire on the laggard tribes: but the measure continues the same, mainly of four stresses to the line. Septs, Heb. p^{e}laggōth, usually translated divisions or channels of water, is more probably sections of the tribe: cf. Nehemiah's use of peleḳ. Read the rest of this line as in the third of verse 16.

16. Sitting between the wattles may have been proverbial like our 'sitting on the fence'. It was a poor thing to listen to the flocks being whistled for, when God's call was abroad.

17. Stayed at home or aloof, Heb. shaken which usually means dwell; but the context here requires its primitive meaning still found in the Arabic sakan, to keep quiet. Truant: the original meanings of the verb, gur, seems to have been to go aside or away, deviate, decline from, and escape (cp. the Arabic), and it is most natural to take it in some such sense here. But as applied to one who left his people to settle among strangers it became the technical term for living as a guest, client, or hireling, among foreigners, and may possibly have that sense here. Dan was neighbour, and apparently subject, to the Phoenicians. Creeks, as if in scorn of Asher's poor harbours. Arabic nouns from the same root mean notches, and inlets in which boats are drawn up.

18. A long 'swell-verse' of five accents, followed by one of three.

19. Kings came, they fought,
Fought the kings of K^{e}ná'an,
At Tá'nák on the streams of M^{e}giddó.
Not a silver-bit took they!
20. From heaven fought the stars,
From their courses they fought with Sis^{e}rá.
22. Then thudded the hoofs of the horses,
Plunge upon plunge of his stallions.
21. Torrent Kishón swept them away,
Onrushing (?) torrent, torrent Kishón.
Forward, my soul, in strength!

23. Curse ye Meróz, saith the LORD [His angel]
Cursing, curse ye her burghers!
For never came they to the help of the LORD,
To the help of the LORD with the brave ones.

24. Blessed above women Ya'él,
Above women in tents be she blessed!
25. Water he craved, milk she gave,
In a dish for lords she brought the curd.
26. Her hand to the peg she put,
Her right to the workman's hammer,
And Sis^{e}rá she hammered, she shattered his head,
She smashed, she hacked through his temples,
27. Between her feet he bent, he fell,
Where he bent there he fell—undone!

19–22. The rush of the battle itself with a change of measure to 3 stresses; with perhaps a 'swell' to 4 in the last line of 19.

22. The context indicates that this verse should lie as above between 20 and 21; both because of the Sis^{e}ra in 20 to which alone *his* stallions can refer; and because of the pronoun them in 21 which has no reference unless preceded by stallions.

21. Swept or gript, Heb. garaph. The same root is used of torrents in Arab. Onrushing (?) torrent, Heb. torrent of Ḳ^{e}dumim. A form of the root in Arabic means forward rushes; so here sudden rises or spates may be more appropriate. The river is subject to these to this day. Others needlessly emending read graves, &c.

23. A quatrain by itself both in measure and subject, 4:3, 4:3. His angel gives a superfluous stress to the first line and is deleted by some for another reason, that it is a later softening of the anthropomorphism. Brave ones, i. e. of Israel (cf. verse 13). Therefore, Meroz, otherwise unknown, was an Israelite town.

24–7. The changing measure is remarkable. After 3 stresses to the line in the opening couplet (24); we have for a slow action 4 (in 25), for a swifter 3 (in 26), and then 4:3 for the deliberate pounding with the hammer, and 4 again for the bend and the fall of Sisera; concluding with a 'swell-line' of 5 on the heavy undone.

24. The text adds 'wife of Heber the Ḳenite', generally recognized as a gloss.

26. The double alliteration and assonance is noteworthy hal^{e}mah, maḥ^{a}ḳah, maḥ^{a}ṣah, ḥal^{e}phah.

27. The text adds a long 5-stressed line—Between her feet he bent, he fell, he lay—which is wanting in eighteen MSS., and all but 'he lay' in eight others; and may be due to dittography. It also makes an odd line.

28. Out of the window she leans, she whines,
Sisᵉrá his mother thorough the lattice:
'Why are his chariots shy to come,
Wherefore tarry the beats of his cars?'
29. Warily answer to her her ladies,
Yea, she returns her words to herself:
30. 'Are they not finding, dividing the spoil?
A wench, two wenches a head for the men,
Booty of dyes for Sisᵉrá,
Booty of dyes with brocade,
Dyes, double brocade, for *my* neck the spoil!'

31. [So perish, O LORD, all Thy foes,
But Thy lovers! like the rise of the sun in his power].

The contrasted pictures of the two women are very powerful; so too the undone chief, and his mother watching greedily for the spoil he is never to bring her: her last thought for her own old neck! And yet some doubt whether the poem was written by a woman.

The rest of the pieces quoted in the Book of Judges are of a kind of verse different in substance from any we have met, and include a Fable and a Riddle.

The Fable is that on Jotham's address to the burghers of Shechem, Judges ix. 7–15, when they had made Abimelech king. The rhythm is little, if at all, removed from that of prose. There is almost no parallelism in the clauses. The prose syntax prevails throughout, there are no inversions of the usual order of words in a clause, nor ellipses nor archaic and purely poetical forms. The measure is mainly of three stresses to the line, with variations to two and four. One couplet remarkably divides between a verb and its object (in verse 15).

28–30. Eleven lines of which the first eight are of 4 stresses to the line, except possibly the fifth, which may have 3. The next two are in 3 each, and the passage closes with a swell-line in 4 (or 5?).

29. Others render: 'the wisest of her ladies.'

30. By changing the position of two words and eliding one Prof. Budde renders the lines more regular—

Booty of a wench, two wenches, each man,
Booty of a dyed thing, two dyed things, for Sisᵉra,
Booty of brocade, two brocades, for my neck.

G. A. Cooke suggests

Are they not finding, dividing the spoil,
A wench, two wenches, for every man,
Spoil of dyed things for Sisᵉrá,
A brocade, two brocades, for my neck!

My neck, Heb. neck of the spoil; Gk. his neck. For the final spoil, ṣhalāl, Ewald and others read shaghal = lady (for the neck of the lady).

31. This couplet in epilogue is perhaps a later addition.

And Yotham went and stood on a headland of Mount Gerizim—the Hebrew has a head, which is not the top, but one of the promontories that run out from the hill over the vale and town of Shechem—and lifted his voice and called, saying:

7. Hearken to me, lords-of-Shᵉkém,
That God may hearken to you!

8. The Trees went their way,
To anoint them a king,
And said to the Olive, Reign o'er us.
9. But to them said the Olive,
Should I leave my fatness
Which gods and men prize,
And go, sway[1] o'er the trees?

10. Then the trees said unto the Fig,
Go thou and reign o'er us!
11. But to them said the Fig,
Should I leave my sweetness,
And my goodly fruit
And go, sway o'er the trees?

12. Then the trees said unto the Vine,
Go thou and reign o'er us,
13. But to them said the Vine,
Should I leave my wine,
That cheers gods and men,
And go, sway o'er the trees?

14. Then said all the trees to the Thorn,
Go thou and reign o'er us!
15. But to them said the Thorn,
If in troth ye anoint
Me to reign over you,[2]
Come trust in my shadow,
But if not, fire shall break from the Thorn,
And consume the cedars of Lᵉbanón.

Of the Riddle, the Ḥīdah,[3] we have one specimen in Judges xiv. 14, set by Samson to the Philistines for a wager. This has always been a favourite amusement, and a form both of friendly and bitter contests, among the peoples of the East. 'To drive the evenings in our now thin and silent company, the old man Nejm propounded riddles over the coffee-hearth. The Arabs were ready, they said

[1] Heb. nu'a, to wave, or swing.

[2] This couplet perhaps ought to be written as one line.

[3] Usually derived from the root ḥid, which in Arabic means to turn from, decline, as if an indirect or 'perverted' or twisted saying in opposition to direct, open speech. Cf. above, p. 55, on Num. xii. 8, where the antithesis of speaking in ḥidoth is mouth to mouth, and openly: marᵉ'ah, what is plain 'at sight'.

theirs, and we guessed round; when the word fell to me, I set them the enigma of the sphinx, saying this was the most famous riddle in the world. . . . When they could not unriddle that dark word-binding of the sphinx, they were delighted with the homely interpretation. Twice again I was taken in riddlers' company in Arabia, and have propounded my riddle since I knew none other: a Beduin weled, son of Oedipus, sitting amongst the second wiseacres, unriddled me at the moment; this kind of parabolical wisdom falls to the Semitic humour and is very pleasant to the Arabs.'[1] It must have been as common among the Hebrews; and as in the cases quoted, so with Samson and with Solomon and the Queen of Sheba, it appears as a natural form of conversation among strangers from different tribes, and between travellers and their hosts.[2] I have heard that riddles are still often set for a wager.

Samson had seen a hive of honey-bees in the dried skin or skeleton of a lion and put his riddle thus—in two lines of three stresses each and with a double alliteration or assonance that is hard to reproduce in English:

Meha'okél yaṣá ma'ᵃkál
Ume'aź yaṣá mathóḳ;

but the folk-tongue in English would have added the obvious rhyme:

From the eater came forth meat,
And from strong came forth sweet.

Delilah gave away the riddle, and when the Philistines answered it in the same measure with the same alliteration in *m*:

Máh-mathóḳ midd^ebásh
Uméh 'aź me'ᵃrí—

What sweeter than honey,
What more strong than a lion?—

he set them another ḥidah (verse 18):

Had not ye ploughed with my heifer,
Ye had not hit on my riddle.

In chapter xv. 16, another verse is attributed to Samson when he slew the Philistines with the jawbone of an ass, lᵉḥī-ḥᵃmor, and it is offered as the origin of Leḥī, the name of the place where he did so. The lines have each two stresses:

With the jaw of an ass,
Heaps upon heaps,
With the jaw of an ass
I slew a thousand of men.

[1] Doughty, *Arabia Deserta*, i. 197.

[2] Ezekiel in xvii. 2 ff. gives a more elaborate ḥidah, developing it into an allegory.

So the Hebrew text. With different vowels the Greek translators read a verb in the second line, and after them one may render

With the jaw of an ass,
In heaps I huddled them.[1]

But the savage humour of the verse lies in this, that the Hebrew for *ass* and for *heaps* and *huddled* have the same consonants; and that from the Aramaic and Arabic as well as from the context these last two would appear to mean heaps of ruins and heap into ruin:

Bil^{e}ḥī ha-ḥ^{a}mōr
ḥ^{a}mor ḥ^{a}martim,

which may be faintly imitated by rendering the whole thus:

With the jaw of an ass
I smashed them in mass;
With the jaw of an ass
Slew a thousand of men.

The last of the Samson verses, ch. xvi. 24, with which the Philistines praised their God when the blinded giant was brought into his temple, has been already given both in Hebrew and English.[2]

In the First Book of Samuel the verses quoted are at least the following:

The Oracle of Samuel to Saul in ch. xv. 22, 23. This must not be overlooked in any appreciation of the early religious distinction of Israel; it holds in germ one of the main principles of later prophecy. The structure is two quatrains of which the couplets are of a longer and a shorter line in the general proportion of 4 : 3; but those of the second quatrain are—in a doubtful text—less regular than those of the first. To reproduce the exact rhythm of the Hebrew is impossible in a language which has no metrical equivalents for the principal terms of the piece. Many must prefer the noble, if somewhat paraphrased, prose of the Authorised Version.

22. Hath Yahwéh delight in things burned and slain
As in obeying the voice of Yahwéh?
Lo, to obey than a slain thing is better,
And to give heed than the fatness of rams.

23. For as the sin of lot-craft is rebellion,
And to presume is as guilt of the idols![3]
As thou hast spurned the word of Yahwéh,
Thee doth He spurn for a king!

1 Heb. *ḥ^{a}mor ḥ^{a}morathaim*, a heap, two heaps = heaps upon heaps. Emend after the Greek *ḥ^{a}mor* (or *ḥomer*) *ḥ^{a}martīm*.

2 Lecture I, p. 24.

3 Heb. 'and the vanity (or wrong) and T^{e}raphim to push' or 'press forward'. But a Greek version reads *as the guilt of T^{e}raphim*, the household or ancestral

Again in xv. 33, the couplet 4 : 3—

Just as women thy sword made childless,
So among women childless thy mother!

The women's acclamation of David in xviii. 7, xxi. 12, xxix. 5; the measure is 3 : 2.

Sha'úl his thousands hath slain,
But Dawíd his thousands ten!

The proverb in xxiv. 14 (Eng. 13), a couplet in 3 : 3. As the ancient proverb saith:

From the wicked wickedness must out,
But never my hand against thee!

We are now almost at the last stage of our survey, the poems ascribed to David or his generation in the Second Book of Samuel.

These are the two elegies on Saul and Jonathan and on Abner, the Cry of the Tribal Revolt from the Kingdom, the great Ode of which Psalm xviii is another edition, and the Rede of David entitled his Last Words. I have already quoted part of the Ode, and will take now the Cry of the Tribes and the Last Words, reserving the elegies to the close as they illustrate one of the striking features of both Arab and early Hebrew poetry, with which it will be most fit to conclude.

The summons to the Revolt of the Tribes from the Kingdom, ch. xx. 1, was given by a Benjamite—bitter, with all the native bitterness of his clan, at their loss of the crown—one Sheba ben-Bechri, described as a man of B^{e}liyyal, anglicized Belial, that is a worthless fellow, who blew a trumpet and called to the northern tribes:

Not to us any share in Dawíd,
Nor heritage ours in son-of-Yishái!
Every man to his tents, Isra'él!

The call is not to war—to take the tents as those of soldiers in the field is a modern inference—nor to an individual anarchy, for it says not his tent but his tents, and is a call to the chiefs of the clans each with his camp. It is the voice of a reaction against the monarchy on the part of that tribal autonomy which Israel brought with them from their desert days. How the habit and the music of the deserts still last in Israel!

images, the family-idols worshipped at that time, 1 Sam. For haphṣer, to push forward, not found elsewhere, some would read ḥepheṣ ra', evil desire. But besides being an awkward phrase this is both against the rhythm and the parallelism.

The 'swan-song' of David, ch. xxiii. 1–7, is a rugged primitive piece carrying no symptom of a late date in its dialect. It is noteworthy that it has the same name of Rede or Oracle, and strikes the same parallel Ia'ᵃḳob-Isra'el, as we found in the Redes of Balaam, which there are other grounds for attributing to this time.[1]

But the author can hardly be David himself; the first two couplets are plainly against this. The measure is mostly of three stresses to the line, with occasional variations to two and here and there a four. There are five stanzas, mainly of two couplets of parallel lines; but there is a remarkable and almost regular occurrence of an odd line.

1. And these the words of Dawíd, the last ones—

Rede of Dawíd, son of Yíshái,
Rede of the yeoman lifted on high,
The christ of the God of Ya'ᵃḳób,
And darling of Israel's chants.

2. Breath of Yahwéh it speaketh by me,
And His the word on my tongue.
3. Hath spoken the God of Ya'ᵃḳób,
To me said the Rock of Isra'el:

Who righteously rules over men,
Who rules in the fear of God,
4. Like morning light he ariseth,
The sun of a cloudless morn,
With the shine and the rain, O the fresh green earth!

5. Is not my house so (?) with God?
Yea, of old He made me a pact,
Ordered throughout and secured.
Yea, all my safety and joy,
Shall He not make it to spring?

1. Darling, Heb. na'īm, H. P. Smith, joy. Such is the more probable meaning, the passive. But others prefer the active, sweet singer. The decision turns not so much on the alternative quality of the form (a–ī) as on the question whether there were two words in Hebrew na'im with a slightly different pronunciation of the middle consonant, as in Arabic na'im = is pleasant, but nagham = to speak softly. This is possible, but both here and in the only other alleged instance of the second sense, Ps. lxxxi. 3, the former meaning is as possible as in other examples of it.

4. By a different division of the lines and the change of one word we get

Like morning light at sunrise,
A morn without clouds and shining,
After the rain, O the greenness of earth!

5. In its context the first line must be read interrogatively. So, some read sure. The last line must also be read as a question: perhaps ki-lo' should be hᵃ-lo.

[1] Above, pp. 70, 71. But Budde and others take the date as very late.

6. But the worthless are all as thorns abhorred,
Not to be taken by hand,
The man that would strike them
Must arm him (?) with iron and spear-shaft,
Till in fire they burning be burned . . .

The only general remark necessary about the two Dirges—the sole specimens of their class among our poems—is that neither breathes the name of God nor hope of another life. In the Dirge on Saul and Jonathan this is most impressive. For there we find a keen relish of life and a most passionate lasting of love, an appreciation of the virtues of the dead and a magnanimous forgiveness of the injuries which one of them had wrought—every instinct proper at the thought of the great dead except the instinct of hope. It may be said, of course, that in the abandonment of grief—grief which is nobly and splendidly passionate in the Dirge on Saul and Jonathan—God and the life to come are naturally forgotten. Yet the silence of these dirges is also the silence of all the narratives and poems through which we have passed; and but illustrates that weird absence of hope which is characteristic of the pagan Arabs and of early Israel even in their mourning for virtuous and beloved men.

The Dirge on Abner, ch. iii. 33, 34, is in six lines of which the first two and the fifth have 2 stresses each, the rest 3. The introduction gives the proper term for making or singing a dirge, ḳonen: and the noun is Ḳinah: how near to our keening! And the king sang a dirge for Abner and said:

As dieth a fool
Must Abner die?
Thy hands unbound and thy feet,
Nor thrust into gyves.
As falleth a fool,
To the lawless fallen art thou!

It is possible that thy feet should be removed to the next line. In the last couplet a fool—necessary both for the rhythm and the sense—is restored from the Greek; the Hebrew text omits it.

The Dirge on Saul and Jonathan, ch. i. 17–27, which is taken from the Book of Yashar, may have suffered like the Song of Deborah from a long oral tradition; or the irregularities of the metre may be original and due to the strong, sobbing passion of the poet. The lines are mainly of 4 stresses each, and here and there a shorter follows a longer as in the true Ḳinah rhythm. Neglecting the parallelism,

6. Worthless, bᵉliyya'al, see above, p. 94. Abhorred, Heb. thrust away or to be thrust away. Arm him, Heb. fill, i.e. load, himself. The last word given in the text to the verse belongs to the following prose.

some print lines of as many as 5 and even 7 stresses and so make six quatrains with a couplet to open and a couplet to close the series. This is possible but we have not yet met with lines of so great a length. I prefer, as in previous poems, to hold to the parallelism and break up these long lines. But again let us remember we have not to do with a written but a chanted song, and the way we arrange the lines does not matter for the music. The title or introduction is unusually long. There is no reason either in the language or the substance of the Dirge to doubt the ascription to David.

And David sang this Dirge—keened this keening—upon Sha'ūl and upon Y^ehonathán his Son; lo! it is Written in the Book of the Valiant, to teach the sons of Y^ehudah hard things, and he said:

19. The Beauty, Isra'el, on thy heights is slain,
How fallen are the heroes!

20. Tell it out not in Gath,
Nor proclaim in 'Ashk^elon's streets;
Lest the Philistines' daughters rejoice,
Lest the daughters of the uncircumcised triumph.

21. Hills of Gilboá', neither dew
Neither rain be upon you, fields of disaster!
For there flung to rust are the bucklers of brave ones,
Shield of Sha'úl, arms of the Anointed.

22. From the blood of the slain,
From the fat of the mighty,
Bow of Y^ehonathán turned not back
Nor clean came home the sword of Sha'úl.

23. Sha'úl and Y^ehonathán, the loved and the dear ones,
In their lives and their death undivided,
They were swifter than eagles,
Than lions more strong.

24. Daughters of Isra'el weep for Sha'úl,
Who clothed you in scarlet with jewels,
Who brought up adorning of gold on your raiment.

17, 18. So transposing the order of the text partly in conformity with similar titles. For the Heb. text ḳesheth, Bow, which gives no sense (some have taken it as the name of a tune), read, by only altering the vowel-points, ḳashoth, Hard things or hardness (the plural for the abstract as often in the O.T.). (Cf. St. Paul, Thou, therefore, endure hardness; lit. suffer evil with.)

19. Beauty or ornament: also the Hebrew name for the gazelle.

20. First line: Al-tagīdu b^egath, with a play upon the name; cf. Micah i. 10.

21. Fields of disaster, reading m^eḥumōth for the t^erumoth of the text; offerings; various conjectures; maweth, death; r^emiyah, deceit, &c. Arms reading k^elē for b^elī. For other readings see the commentaries.

25. How fallen are the heroes
In the thick of the battle!

Y^e^honathán on thy heights [thou art] slain,
26. Anguish is mine for thee!
O my brother, Y^e^honathán!
Dearest thou wert to me,
Thy love to me was wonderful,
Passing the love of women.

27. How fallen are the heroes,
And perished war's weapons!

Of the material for our subject, as defined in the Introduction to these Lectures, there remains only the fragment attributed to Solomon at the opening of the Temple.[1]

This has come down to us in two forms: one in Hebrew (1 Kings viii. 12, 13), and one in Greek, inserted out of place after verse 53 of the same chapter, with the addition: Behold, is it not written in the Book of the Song; the Hebrew for which was Sepher hash-Shír —perhaps an inversion of the name hay-Yashar.[2]

The Hebrew is in three lines, 4 : 4 : 3—

Yahweh 'amar lishkōn ba'^{a}raphĕl
Banoh banīthī beth z^{e}bul lak
Makōn l^{e}shibt^{e}ka 'ōlamīm,

which literally translated runs thus:

Yahweh decreed to dwell in the storm-cloud;
Building I've built Thee a lofty house,[3]
Seat for Thy dwelling for ever.

The Greek edition gives four lines, of which the first is new, with probably this Hebrew behind it:

hash-Shemesh hekīn bash-shamaim Yahweh,

and the other three are based, with variations, on the Hebrew, the whole running 4 : 3 : 4 : 2 thus:

The Sun in the heavens Yahweh hath set,
Decreed to dwell in the storm-cloud [Himself].

[1] The Cry of the Tribes in Revolt from David's Dynasty, 1 Kings xii. 16, has already been treated on p. 94; its use by a Benjamite, 2 Sam. xx. 1.

[2] So Wellhausen. See above, Introduction.

[3] Beth z^{e}bul. In late Heb. z^{e}bul = Temple. Some take it to mean simply a dwelling, but others compare the Assyr. bit zabal = lofty house. (Schrader, *Cuneiform Inscr. and the O. T.*, 174, 175.) Cf. Isa. lxiii. 16, where it is used of Yahweh's dwelling, as if high or sublime abode; and Hab. iii. 11, where it is the lofty stations of the sun and moon.

Build thou my House, eminent House for Thyself[1] (*sic*)
To dwell in for ever.

The last two lines, however, are finer in the Hebrew text; they yield a more regular metre, and the Greek itself bears evidence to their originality.[2] We may, therefore, take the whole in this form, 4 : 3 : 4 : 3—

The Sun in the heavens Yahweh hath set,
Decreeing to dwell in the storm-cloud [Himself].
I have built now for Thee a lofty abode,
A seat for Thy dwelling for ever.

If Wellhausen's emendation of the Greek appendix to the lines be accepted, and if they were taken from the Book of Yashar—the same source to which we owe Joshua's address to Sun and Moon and David's Dirge—then their high antiquity is assured. If not Solomon's own, they cannot be much later than his time. As such they are very valuable: Israel's Creed, when the nation had built their Temple and assembling in the court before it under the heavens, directed their worship not to the open glories of these but to Him who having created all things visible, Himself remained unseen and inscrutable, the Inhabitant of the darkness of the storm-cloud, as their fathers had told them, for whose dwelling among themselves they had therefore prepared that dark and empty chamber in front of them.[3]

[1] *Οἶκον ἐκπρεπῆ σαυτῷ* (so Cod. B), evidently a translation of the Hebrew beth z^e^bul lak. But Cod. A has the reading *εὐπρεπῆ*, seemly, Heb. na'weh, which may be taken as a misreading for naweh, dwelling; and the line translated, Build Me a house, a homestead for Me. So virtually Wellhausen; but this requires the reading *ἐμοί* (Heb. lī) instead of *σαυτῷ* (Heb. lak), which conflicts with the first clause of the same line. By its preservation of *σαυτῷ* (lak), in spite of the preceding clause, the Greek affords striking testimony to the superiority in the last two lines of the Hebrew edition.

[2] See end of preceding note.

[3] See further the author's *Jerusalem*, vol. ii, 74, 75.

INDEX OF PASSAGES

*** A list of all the poetical pieces treated in the Lectures is given on the first and second pages of the Introduction.

www.ingramcontent.com/pod-product-compliance
Lightning Source LLC
Chambersburg PA
CBHW071143090426
42736CB00012B/2211
9781606082430